Letter
From Alabama

The Inspiring True Story of Strangers Who Saved a Child and Changed a Family Forever

By David L. Workman

Version 3

Also available as an Ebook
ISBN: 978-0-9962309-0-2

Stay in touch for updates:

https://www.facebook.com/letterfromalabama

www.workman-inc.com

letter-from-alabama@comcast.net

Special Acknowledgements

The author gives special thanks to Clover; to daughters Kara Elisabeth and Kirsten Cynthia; to stepdaughters Laura and Lynn; to sons-in-law Tim and Paul and Brian; to Dustin; to grandchildren Taryn and Adria, Devon and Marlee, John David and Ruby; to legions of friends and loved ones. You inspire and encourage me; you make me laugh; and you make life a rich blessing and adventure in a crazy and sometimes ugly, but ultimately beautiful, world. From the bottom of my heart, I thank you.

The author also is indebted to those who lived the events described here, and to those who heard first-hand accounts from those who did. Thank you for taking the care to help me recall the events, to review my descriptions, to indulge my many phone calls and emails, and to offer your irreplaceable assistance in retelling the story as accurately as humanly possible. Thank you, brother Dan Welch, sister-in-law Mickey Workman, brother-in-law Dan Quinn, cousin Marilyn Slusser, cousin Sam Laswell, mentor and friend Ralph Langer, and late-in-life friend Carl Smith—grandson of Luella Smith, without whom this story would have a very different ending.

And thank you, Dan Welch, for selflessly sharing your wonderful mother Louise—for opening your great heart and embracing me from the very beginning as your true brother.

Thank you, graphic artist, and friend and colleague, Luis Prado for thoroughly understanding the story of *Letter from Alabama* and then creating a superb cover and maps that perfectly reveal what this book is about.

Table of Contents

Why This Story
Is Written

This is the story of a little boy and an infant girl abandoned, and of a family and complete strangers who acted to save them both.

It's the story of human failure, and human triumph. Forgiveness and redemption.

This story is written as a testament to, and a prayer of thanks for, good and decent people everywhere who stand up for a child when they don't have to—when they have nothing to gain and perhaps much to lose.

It's a tribute to those who see the potential in a young person and give that person a chance to be the best that he or she can be. They are the heroes for whom this story is now committed to writing.

David L. Workman
Olympia, Washington
United States of America
February 2015

The Day that Will Change Everything

March 23, 1950, seems very normal in north-central Ohio's Richland, Ashland and Holmes counties. The Mansfield News–Journal, one of the major sources of timely news for this region, will record temperatures in the 30s in the morning, and edging upwards at noon.

Numerous people will see their names in the paper, as patients at General Hospital and People's Hospital. Death has claimed several people in the area—some from natural causes and two in a car-truck collision in nearby Galion. Six babies were born yesterday at General Hospital.

"Twelve O'Clock High" is showing at the Madison Theater; "Tornado Range" and "Chicago Deadline" are at the Park Theater; "I Stole a Million" and "The Secret Garden" are at the Ritz.

Tonight, the Free and Accepted Masons Lodge is meeting, as are the Catholic Order of Foresters, the Order of Owls, the Knights of Pythias, the Mansfield Model Airplane Club, and the 37th Division Association of the Veterans of Foreign Wars.

So it goes in this city of 43,500 people, which is the seat of government for Richland County and a major go-to place for shopping and other services, among the small towns in the surrounding countryside. Including Loudonville.

In the village of Loudonville, 21 miles to the southeast of Mansfield on State Route 39, Hortense Laswell is a 43-year-old mother of four who grew up in this country and recently moved back with three of her four sons and her new husband George. This morning, she tells 17-year-old son Gene and 13-year-old Jack that she will be driving today to Mount Vernon to bake cookies with Aunt Grace.

This, too, is quite normal, although momentous.

In Hortense's family, Grace Berry Koppert occupies a very special place in the family. She will always be known as Aunt Grace, although on a standard family tree drawing, she would show up as a cousin. For much of Hortense's childhood and adolescence, Grace was the closest person Hortense had to a mother.

Their bond was established soon after Hortense's mother, Della (or Delphina), died tragically on Nov. 10, 1906.

Della Spreng had married Frederick Huffman in 1898 in Loudonville. Della and Fred were a young couple living on one of the Huffman family farms in Washington Township, Holmes County, just outside Loudonville. On the farms and in nearby towns and townships lived members of their extended families, who were immigrants or descendants of immigrants from the Alsace region of France.

In 1906, Della was pregnant, and as her due date approached, there was growing excitement among the Alsatian-American families in the Loudonville area. Della's and Fred's child would add another life to the extended group of cousins, aunts and uncles in this part of Ohio.

In October 1906, the doctor was called to the Huffman farm to help deliver Della's child. In these times in rural communities across America, it was common for doctors to visit and care for their patients at home.

Exactly what happened that day is not officially recorded, but the story will still be remembered a century later in Della's and Fred's family. As the story has been passed down, the doctor was compromised by alcohol, and he delivered a little girl whose name would be Hortense Huffman. What the doctor did not realize, according to the family memory, is that Hortense was a twin—as was her father Fred.

The doctor failed to deliver Hortense's twin, who remained in the womb. When the dreadful error was discovered, it was too late. The second baby girl was dead, and Della was dangerously ill from blood poisoning.

The little body of Hortense's twin sister was buried in the orchard on Fred Huffman's hillside farm.

Three weeks later, on November 9, 1906, tragedy struck again. The Loudonville newspaper reported: "The community was greatly shocked last Saturday morning to hear of the death of Mrs. Fred Huffman. She had passed through a serious illness and was gaining strength and while the physicians could not yet hold out much hope, the family was much encouraged and looking for her recovery. Friday evening, she expressed a wish to sit up a little while, which wish was granted. She was soon afterwards seized with a chill and sank rapidly, her young life coming to a close on earth at 7:15 o'clock Saturday morning and her soul returning to her savior."

The obituary continued: "To the motherless babe, needing so much the mother's care, to the grief stricken husband and to the large circle of relatives and friends in this hour of bereavement is extended the sympathy of the community. God above can offer satisfying consolation. May his peaceful benediction be upon you."

Suddenly, Fred had become a young father solely responsible for an infant daughter; in his grief, he would have to find a way to go on without his young wife, Della.

At times such as these, there can be strength and solace in numbers; and so it was among the Alsatian-American families in the Loudonville-Nashville area of Ohio at the beginning of the 20th century.

Among the network of relatives, Fred would find exactly the right nanny for his new child, Hortense. Grace Berry is 21 years old at the time, and for the next 16 years, she is the person who will help Fred bring up and nurture Hortense.

Grace—"Aunt Grace" as she will forever afterward be known in Hortense's family—will become a surrogate mother to the child. Ironically, Grace will never give birth to children of her own, even after marrying Bill Koppert.

Although Hortense's father eventually finds a new wife during Hortense's teen years, Aunt Grace will always retain her special place in the hearts of Hortense and her family.

As a child, Hortense is baptized into the Christian faith at Trinity Evangelical Church in Loudonville, where Huffmans and Heffelfingers and many other related families fill the pews on Sunday morning.

Each of her children will be baptized here as well.

Hortense will grow up loved and encouraged and watched over by countless grandparents, uncles, aunts, cousins, and friends. Not to mention Fred Huffman and Grace Berry Koppert.

In 1997, Loudonville High School classmate Harold Obrecht will recall Hortense as a good student and a friendly person who was easy to talk to, well-liked and respected at school. Both of them will graduate among the 33-member Class of 1924. In such a small class, the students get to know each other very well during four years together in high school.

At age 18, soon after graduating, Hortense marries a tall, slender, good-looking fellow who is the son and grandson of respected businessmen in Loudonville. His name is Ralph O. Workman.

Ralph's father is a successful local merchant. Ralph's paternal grandfather William Workman, by now deceased, was a farmer and a minister in the local Dunkard—or Brethren—Church. His maternal grandfather David Stacher, also deceased, was a farmer and businessman who co-founded Loudonville's first bank.

Ralph is descended from one of the original founders of Loudonville—James Loudon Priest. He and his mother Viola are descended from Melchior Stacher who emigrated from Germany to Pennsylvania in the American colonies in 1732. Ralph is descended from Workmans who migrated from the Netherlands in 1647 to a colony that was then named New Amsterdam, and later New York.

His Grandfather and Grandmother Stacher were the ones who built a prosperous farm on the gentle hill on East Main Street at the edge of Loudonville in about 1880. The graceful farmhouse, the two-story barn, and assorted outbuildings will become an integral part of the life story and life experience of Ralph's and Hortense's children and grandchildren. Yet Ralph and Hortense themselves never live at the farm together.

When Ralph and Hortense marry in 1924, a wedding gift from Ralph's parents—Harry and Viola Workman—is a new home that is built for them in town, within an easy stroll of schools and church and Loudonville's downtown shops. The newlyweds' house is directly across the street from Harry and Viola.

Over the next dozen years, Hortense and Ralph create a household and a business. First come Ralph Jr. in 1926, then Gene in 1933 and Jack in 1936.

Ralph Sr. and his father start a dairy, bottling and delivering Guernsey milk products, and the two oldest boys will remember Hortense washing the milk bottles in the kitchen sink in the early days of the enterprise.

In time, business is good enough that summer vacations become viable for Ralph Sr., Hortense and the three boys. Ralph Jr. and Gene will remember a winter trip to Florida with their mom and dad. Unfortunately, as it will turn out, the vacations often will be times of separation rather than togetherness. Hortense will take Junior, Gene and Jack to Michigan in an effort to escape the little-understood environmental factors that trigger Junior's severe childhood asthma attacks. On at least one occasion, in 1938, Ralph Sr. will make a trip to Florida with friends.[i]

And then, about 1940, it ends. On Ralph Sr.'s business trips to Cleveland, he meets a vivacious woman named Marie and falls in love—a love that will last the rest of his life. He announces his intention to divorce Hortense—something that, in small Ohio towns before World War II, is far from common.

Gene will later say, "I grew up in a broken home long before there were broken homes."[ii]

One of Ralph Sr.'s treasured possessions will be a 1940 photo of himself and Marie at a bar in Havana, Cuba. They're a very attractive couple. Unfortunately for Hortense and the three boys, the four of them are on their own from here on.

In Loudonville, the divorce of Ralph Sr. and Hortense comes as a jolt that will be remembered around town, and in the extended families, for decades to come.

The breakup, coming as the clouds of war are forming over Europe and the Pacific, will leave Hortense in a terrible predicament. In addition to the emotional roller-coaster that she surely endures, she also has to confront the reality of providing for her sons with whatever support she can get from Ralph Sr., which isn't always forthcoming.

Even for a high school graduate, Loudonville in the early 1940s isn't a magnet for family-wage jobs for women. With help from Aunt Grace, Hortense—mother of three sons—takes the bus to and from Wooster for classes at Wooster Business College. There, she will acquire the knowledge and keypunch skills for the early era of data processing—a revolution that will arrive in full force long after her death.

Hortense emerges with a certificate qualifying her to operate International Business Machines punch card machines.

Now, the question is where can she put her business machine skills to work? Not Loudonville. Not Mansfield or Ashland or Wooster. Not even Cleveland.

In 1942 or the beginning of 1943, when Hortense is 36 years old, America's massive War Production buildup calls the new graduate-divorcee-mother to Dayton, Ohio—home of three military airfields.

When Hortense moves to Dayton with Gene and Jack, the fateful day of March 23, 1950, is still unimaginably far in the future. When that day comes, an entire family will be forever changed.

First, however, there is an entire World War to live through, and to win. The small-town girl from an Alsatian enclave in Ohio will do her part to help win the most massive and destructive war in the history of the world. She will meet people who will change her life.

And somewhere in Dayton, Hortense will make a friend or an acquaintance who will one day read a letter from

Alabama. This letter, and its effect, will be little short of a miracle in the lives of Hortense's loved ones.

The brothers—Ralph Jr., Jack and Gene—early 1940s

—2—
The Boy from Mount Vernon

No one who is alive in the second decade of the 21st century knows whether George Shelton Laswell saw irony in how his life would change on that March day in 1950 when Hortense sent her middle two sons, Gene and Jack, off to school in Loudonville and drove down Route 3 through the rolling hills and forests and farms to Mount Vernon, Ohio, to bake cookies.

George had come into this world in June 1913, in Mount Vernon, Kentucky, the seat of government for the Bluegrass State's Rockcastle County.

Mount Vernon, Ohio, is the county seat of the Buckeye State's Knox County. In a very important way, this is where his life will change forever.

Both Mount Vernons are picturesque hubs for rural areas in their respective regions. Both are named for the Virginia plantation home of America's first president.

Both towns abide in the east-central, hilly regions of their states. Both reflect some of America's small-town values and experience.

Like Hortense, George sprang from rural roots. All of Hortense's Alsatian great-grandparents immigrated to Ohio from villages in the Vosges / Rhine region of France in the 1820s and 1830s. That was a time when thousands of desperate Alsatians fled the economic destruction growing out of the Napoleonic Wars.

George's roots in America extend back to early colonial days. One of his ancestors was very possibly the immigrant William Lasswell, who left England to settle land that he purchased in colonial New Jersey in 1664. In the next century, an "s" would be lost from the family name.

George's ancestors—Laswells, Clarks, Abneys and others—were also among the earliest white settlers of Kentucky, traveling by foot and horseback, and later by wagon, over the pioneers' Wilderness Road in the final two decades of the 1700s and the years soon after 1800. It is likely that some of them knew the legendary frontiersman, Daniel Boone, and his family. Some of them fought in the American War for Independence.

Whereas Hortense is the only surviving child of the late Fred and Della Huffman, George is one of 15 children of physician and farmer William David Laswell, who reared his family in Lincoln County, Kentucky, in a settlement known as Kings Mountain.

Like Loudonville, Ohio, Kings Mountain was, at one time, a bustling little railroad town. It was a stop on the Southern Railway, where a tunnel bored through one of the hills.

George's father was known as Dr. Laswell, a country physician and surgeon who received his medical degree in Louisville in 1904. Dr. Laswell also owned substantial farming operations and an early local telephone system. Judging from the written accounts of the time, Dr. Laswell was a well-regarded and prosperous member of the Lincoln County community.

The Laswell home in Kings Mountain was large for a little town, and also served as the office for his medical practice. Dr. Laswell's children and grandchildren would later describe the house as full of people.

If George grew up in a respected and prosperous family, he also has known his share of loss and hardship, starting soon after birth, when his mother died a horrible death, the details of which would become known to Hortense's family much later. Then, when George was 15, his stepmother died in childbirth.

In the World War II and postwar years of the 1940s and 1950s, the factories and the humming economy of Ohio's manufacturing cities and towns attract and employ lots of young men and women and families from south of the Ohio River.

Unlike many of these people seeking a better life and a family income, George isn't drawn to factories or unionized jobs.

Throughout his adult life, he seems to gravitate to delivery jobs and landscaping / nursery work. That is, when he has work . . .

Sometime between 1945 and 1948, George lands in Dayton, where he meets a sweet, hard-working, well-educated older woman with three sons. Her name is Hortense Workman.

Hortense

George with nephew Glenn
Laswell in 1947

—3—
Strangers in a Strange City

As an adult, Gene Workman will recall what a culture shock Dayton represented in his young life when his mother moved herself and two of the boys there in the 1940s. For the first 10 years of his life, he lived in a village where everything he wanted or needed to do was within walking distance, and where he had friends and cousins all around. Not to mention grandparents, great-aunts and great-uncles. In Loudonville, he had fields and pastures and woods to explore, swimming holes to dive into, and hills to roam in all directions.

By contrast, Dayton is big, noisy, and busy. Going anywhere means riding an electric trolley down the urban streets. In a strange city, the 10-year-old from Loudonville is a stranger.

At this time when the United States and its Allies are at war with Japan and Germany and Italy, Dayton is home to numerous factories of major corporations, including NCR (National Cash Register); DELCO (co-founded as Dayton Engineering Laboratories Company by one of Loudonville's native sons, Charles Kettering); and General Motors divisions, including Frigidaire and Inland Manufacturing.

It is a technology center in much the way that Silicon Valley will one day be America's high-tech innovation capital.

Not coincidentally, Dayton is Ground Zero for America's aviation industry, where two brothers named Orville and Wilbur Wright expanded from building bicycles to inventing and manufacturing airplanes in the early years of the century.

By the beginning of World War II, the Dayton area has three air fields—Wright Field, Patterson Field, and McCook Field. Two of them will become better known as Wright-Patterson Air Force Base in 1948.

This aviation and manufacturing base equips Dayton to become an important part of America's single-minded focus on defeating the Axis Powers in World War II, and bringing America's soldier, sailors and aviators home.

In no small measure, the Allies' victory in World War II will be attributable to America's astounding War Production effort. President Franklin D. Roosevelt and his administration quite simply organize and incentivize American industry to turn out the weapons, equipment and other material required by the Allies' fighting forces to defeat the Nazis, Japan and Fascist Italy.

In Dayton, this means that 61 primary war production industries will employ 115,000 workers by 1943.[iii]

One of those workers is Hortense Workman, from Loudonville, Ohio. Armed with her educational credential from Wooster Business College, certifying that she is qualified to operate the state-of-the-art punch-card data processing equipment of International Business Machines (IBM), Hortense has found a job that will help her support herself, Gene, Jack and, to a lesser extent, Ralph Jr., who has chosen to strike out on his own as a teenager following his parents' divorce.

Hortense's new employer is Frigidaire, a division of GM. Like other major U.S. industrial companies, Frigidaire has put consumer production on hold and is now gearing up to produce an arsenal of weaponry products for the United States government rather than refrigerators or clothes washers or dishwasher components for the homes of America and the world. Frigidaire's wartime weaponry will include airplane propeller parts and assemblies, aircraft machine guns, aircraft control valves, aircraft fuel tanks, bomb cases and hangers, bullet cores, carburetors, diesel engine parts, hydraulic switches, tank track assemblies, and water-cooled machine guns.[iv]

In her job at Frigidaire, Hortense undoubtedly sees the posters promoting work place safety. There is good reason for this emphasis on safety. During the frantic push to produce what is needed to win a world war, more Americans will be killed or disabled in work place accidents than on the battlefields between 1941 and 1945.[v]

While the industrial buildup is accelerating in Dayton, the Army Air Corps doubles the size of Wright Field, greatly enlarges Patterson Field, and constructs a headquarters for the new Air Service Command. By 1943, military employment at Wright, Patterson and McCook air fields will approach 45,000.[vi]

One of the bulldozer operators who make this expansion happen is a swarthy, strong young Kentuckian named Ernie Muse. He will remember wearing a sidearm on his hip while grading the earth to make way for the expansion of the airfield. The pistol is standard equipment for the dozer operators, so they can shoot the remaining rattlesnakes that occupy the prairie grassland outside Dayton.

Later, Ernie will become an important person in the lives of Hortense's family.

To accommodate the influx of civilian and military defense workers, Dayton has to change. Most urgent is the need for new housing for defense workers and their young families. The shortage of existing housing drives rents up, and this leads to federal rent controls when voluntary persuasion fails.

The housing shortage also leads the federal government and the Dayton Council for Defense to begin the construction of subsidized rental apartments. The largest of these is Overlook Homes on the eastern edge of Dayton near the military airfields.

The first defense-worker families move into the one-story barracks-style Overlook apartments in December 1942. Hortense and nine-year-old Gene and six-year-old Jack are among the first occupants. A cousin of Hortense's will later remember the apartment on Vandergrift Drive as tiny—a far cry from the family homes back in Loudonville. For a single mother struggling to earn a living, care for her boys and make ends meet, it will do. With help from family friend and housekeeper

Rhea Stouffer from Loudonville, Hortense and the boys make the apartment work.

During the Workman family's six years in Dayton, Gene will feel that he is saved and grounded by two great, positive influences on his life.

One is Boy Scouting, where he will find good male role models and acquire values, skills and practical outdoor knowledge to last a lifetime and build a foundation for his future. Hortense even makes time to serve as a Den Leader for Gene and several other boys when he starts the first phase of Scouting, known as Cub Scouts.

The other positive influence is a farm at Fort Recovery, Ohio, where Hortense's Aunt Pearl and Uncle Lew raise livestock and grow a variety of crops suitable for animals and human consumption. During the Dayton years, Gene spends his summers at the Fort Recovery farm on the flat, glacier-smoothed plains of west-central Ohio.

After Uncle Lew dies and the farm passes into the hands of Hortense's cousin Irma and her husband, Irvin, Gene resumes his summers there. He works the fields and tends to the animals, and feels deeply rooted to the land. At heart, Gene is, and always will be, a farm boy.

Irma and Irvin and their older children love the times when Gene comes to live and work with them. He becomes the children's "big brother," whom they will love dearly for the rest of their lives.

Gene and his future wife will always stay in touch with the cousins in Fort Recovery, visiting them at every opportunity in the years to come. And they, in turn, will visit Gene and his family on trips to north-central and northeast Ohio.

Meanwhile, Hortense's oldest son, Ralph Jr., makes his way in the world after leaving home following his parents' divorce. Starting out as a self-supporting teenager in the big Lake Erie city of Cleveland, Ralph eventually lands and settles in Springfield, a few miles northeast of Dayton. In the process, Junior accumulates a lifetime of stories that he will, on occasion, retell in the form of life lessons for the children he will choose to rear into adulthood.

Long lost from the family memory is the story of how and where, and under what circumstances, Hortense Workman meets George Laswell in Dayton.

What is known is that, sometime after his father's death in Kentucky in 1945, George migrates across the Ohio River into Cincinnati and then up U.S. 48 to Dayton. Or perhaps he takes the train or bus. By this time, Hortense and Gene and Jack have been in Dayton for a few years, or perhaps several.

Unlike Hortense, it seems that George doesn't land a job with one of the big industries in his new home town. What is certain is that he works as a driver for a food service company for a while.[vii]

Whenever and however they meet, the 40-something mother of three sons and the 30-something single man must feel they have a great deal in common.

Both lost their mothers soon after being born. Both had the experience of losing a "second mother." In George's case, his father's second wife died in childbirth. In Hortense's case, Aunt Grace—the cousin who helped her father rear her as a nanny—was replaced by her father's second wife, Agnes, when Hortense was in high school.

Hortense and George have come from small rural towns where everybody knows everybody.

At some point in the 1940s, while in Dayton, Hortense has another male friend who is important enough that she introduces him to her cousins at Fort Recovery. However, George Laswell is the man with whom she becomes very serious.

George is blue-eyed, ruddy-complexioned, slender of build and standing five feet, seven inches tall. He has a full head of light-brownish hair.[viii]

Hortense is slender with a pleasing countenance. Photos of her at age 40 or so show her wearing her curled brown hair halfway to her shoulders. She is always in a dress. Her face is rather narrow, her eyes dark, her teeth well formed. Her

25 |

smooth skin has cheek creases that her youngest son will inherit.

And then, in 1948, Hortense and George learn that they are about to become parents together. Twelve and a half years after giving birth to Jack, her youngest, Hortense will be giving birth again. About this time, Hortense and George are married.

The little apartment in Overlook Homes gains another occupant when George moves in. One more is on the way.

—4—
A Child Is Born

On an unusually balmy winter day in 1949, when the outside temperature is 50 degrees Fahrenheit instead of the typical 20 or 30, Hortense's time has come. She leaves Overlook Homes and makes the 5½-mile trip to Miami Valley Hospital.

Hopefully, George—the father-to-be and husband—helps her into the vehicle and drives her down Vandergrift Drive to Airway Road, right on East Third Street, then left on Patterson Boulevard to South Main Street, where Dayton's 69-year-old, state-of-the-art regional hospital awaits them. The expectant mother is checked in, and taken to Room 269.

It has been 40 weeks since a new life was conceived within Hortense. Now, at 19 minutes after 2 o'clock on a Friday morning, while most of Dayton sleeps, a child comes screaming into this world—all 9 pounds and 14 ounces of him.

This event is not of major consequence in Dayton, Ohio.

On this day, Dayton newspaper readers learn of the massive search for a missing 3-year-old child in Reading, Pennsylvania. According to the newspaper report, "National Guard airmen flew over the scene. Firemen, soldiers, Boy Scouts, neighbors and state police joined the hunt . . . ." In all, a thousand searchers are scouring the area for the little blond boy who was last seen wearing a bright red cap.

Meanwhile, President Harry Truman is making the case in the newspapers for the North Atlantic Treaty Organization—the mutual-security agreement of Western Bloc nations that will keep hundreds of thousands of American troops on European soil for decades and eventually win what will be known as the Cold War. This news also occupies a space on Page 1 of the Dayton Daily News.

And in White Plains, New York, 29-year-old Gerard Graham Dennis is being held by police there as the suspected "million dollar jewel thief" who has allegedly carried out a string of successful burglaries in New York state and in California. In Dayton, Ohio, this scintillating news gets top billing in the afternoon newspaper.

It is not big news that another baby, even a 9-pound, 14-ounce one, has been born in Miami Valley Hospital. A time will come, however, when Hortense's youngest son's name will appear in the pages of Dayton's morning newspaper.

Hortense's newborn son will one day thank heaven for the newspapers of Dayton, Ohio, operated and inspired by James Middleton Cox Sr., former Ohio governor, former congressman, and former Democratic nominee for the presidency of the United States of America.

The newborn child's name will be David Lee Laswell. Why he is so named will be a mystery to David for a long time to come.

The Certificate of Live Birth signed by Dr. Cass will, over time, speak volumes to David. It will tell him what little he knows about his first moments on this earth as a separate human being, and about the people who brought him into the world.

At 42 years of age, Hortense has a fourth son, who joins brothers Ralph, turning 23 years old; Gene, turning 16; and Jack, 12. After delivering another big baby into this world, Hortense must be exhausted. And things will not improve in that department.

In the winter of 1949, with a new child arrived, big adjustments are in store for Hortense, George and family.

At 35 years of age, George Laswell suddenly has huge responsibilities. He is not only a husband and stepfather, but he is also a father. His new family will need to count on him to be a major breadwinner. Hortense's days as a defense worker at Wright Field / Wright-Patterson Air Force Base have come to an end, and the new family will be leaving Overlook Homes and Dayton.

Meanwhile, with a new baby in the household, there are cloth diapers to change and rinse and wash. Disposable paper diapers are not yet an option for the parents of America.

Life with a new baby must surely change the dynamic in Hortense's and George's new household. There is a soft "bottom" to wipe, and a squirming little ball of baby fat to bathe. There are seemingly endless hours of feedings. There are blessed hours when David is asleep, followed outbursts of shrill crying and wrinkled little legs kicking when we awakes to demand attention. There are tiny, growing fingernails and toenails to trim.

There is so much to do in this newly combined, growing family.

A picture from this time speaks volumes. A few days after giving birth, Hortense is on a couch holding little David in her arms and looking down at him. She seems to be in distress. He appears to be screaming at the top of his lungs. One can only sympathize with this mother who has so many people depending on her.

In the little apartment, there is precious little space for all of this activity. Soon, however, the cramped quarters won't be among the issues that Hortense's and George's blended family will contend with.

As the 1948-49 school year in Dayton winds to a close, George and Hortense and the boys—Gene and Jack—are packing to move. Little David is going along for the ride.

After several years in Dayton, supporting the Army Air Corps, Hortense will return with her family to Loudonville on the bank of the Mohican River in the hills and forests and farm country of a part of Ohio that, for some, is truly "God's country."

It is a move "back home" for Hortense and her older boys. It is a move to a new world for George Laswell. For George, life is about to become very, very different, in ways he can scarcely imagine.

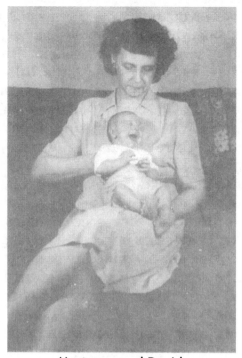

Hortense and David

—5—
Back Home Again

One day in early June of 1949, after Gene and Jack have finished another year of school in Dayton, Hortense and George load up the three boys and the possessions that the family can take with them, and they point their car towards Loudonville.

Sometime before heading out of town, they almost certainly drive up to the gasoline pump at a nearby service station.

A uniformed attendant is waiting for them. The driver—most likely, George—turns off the ignition. He takes hold of a hand crank in the driver's-side car door, turns the crank several times, thus lowering the window.

George, if he is the driver, tells the attendant how much gas to pump. The attendant pumps it, and washes the windshield, and lifts the hood to check the oil level. If the car needs oil, the attendant tops it off.

And then the attendant returns to the driver's open window. It's time to collect the money, and for this purpose the attendant wears a coin-holder device on his belt. It has four cylinders, each stacked with quarters or dimes or nickels or pennies. With this device, he is well equipped for taking money and giving change. George and Hortense pay the attendant the whopping price of about 17 cents per gallon.[ix]

Ten gallons will cost $1.70. In 1949, this is real money. They give the attendant cash or coin. If they have any change coming, he—always a he—gives it to them as they wait in the car.

This is how gasoline service stations operate in Ohio in the middle of the 20th century. There is no such thing as "self service" at the gas pump. The driver never even has to leave the car, unless it's to use the public restroom, or get something out of the trunk.

In this era before Dwight Eisenhower is President of the United States and seven years before he signs the National Interstate and Defense Highways Act, there is no freeway system to speed cars and trucks from one part of America, or one part of Ohio, to another.

Highways are mostly two-lane affairs—no medians—with traffic going and coming in opposite directions, stopping and going in every sizable town along the way.

On this, his first trip to Loudonville, infant Davy is aware only of the inside of the car—and the people in it who can hold, feed and humor him. On many trips to Loudonville in the years to come, the landmarks along the way will comfort and encourage the growing boy. Each will say to him: "You're getting closer!"

In 1949, a likely route for Hortense and George and their family from Dayton is to take State Route 4 northeast to Springfield, then to Mechanicsburg, and from there to Marysville. Here, the route to Loudonville shifts to U.S. 36, eastward to the village of Sunbury at Delaware, named for one of the Indian nations that occupied this region at the time of white settlement. From Delaware, the route resumes a northeastward course on State Route 3 to Mount Vernon, where the old highway makes a roundabout at the towering Civil War Veterans Monument, then on past the Seventh Day Adventist academy, and across the hilly countryside leading to Loudonville.

Along the way, they pass barns neatly painted in black with white lettering:

CHEW
MAIL POUCH TOBACCO
TREAT YOURSELF TO THE BEST

In the 20th century, thousands of barns are painted with this advertisement, giving farm families a free, fresh coat of paint for their barns every now and then.

It's likely that Hortense and her family stop in Mount Vernon to visit briefly with Aunt Grace. Any trip through Mount Vernon is a welcome opportunity to spend a little time with the sweet lady who means so much to Hortense and her family. Aunt Grace loves it when they stop.

Fourteen miles beyond Mount Vernon, where Route 3 converges with State Route 205, the family comes to Jelloway. Although it is but a wide spot in the road, with its own cemetery, Jelloway is a welcome sight on a trip to Loudonville because it means you are only eight miles away.

More than a century before this trip in 1949, a group of Workman pioneers stopped their wagons and settled near here. They carried the money (hard cash) that they received for their land in Maryland. The cash was in barrels, which they hid under the roof of the porch of their newly built cabin.[x]

By about 1840, Workmans had migrated again and were living just outside Loudonville, along Route 3 towards Wooster. Their Loudonville settlement was known as Plum Run, for the tiny tributary to the Mohican River. Into the 21st century, it will be marked by a cemetery with ancient, weathered tombstones.

In mid-20th century, when Hortense and her family return home from Dayton, Loudonville is changing.

Farming is still a mainstay, but many of the old homesteaders' farms have failed—and with them, the depleted and eroded soils. The remaining farms produce livestock, poultry, wheat, corn and just about any crop that grows in the temperate climate of the Great Lakes states.

Loudonville's flour mill continues to process the hard wheat from the surrounding region into cracker flour. A mill has operated here since 1818 and will into the 21st century.

Loudonville's home-grown Flxible Company, originally founded to manufacture the flexible couplings for motorcycle sidecars, is now operating in a modern factory—turning out funeral hearses, ambulances and buses. In the decades to come, it will be purchased more than once before being shut down in 1996.[xi]

As time passes, more and more of the farms in the area will be purchased by Amish people—an Anabaptist Christian sect from Western Europe. With their simpler ways and minimal reliance on modern contraptions, they will be able to make a living from farms long after the original farm families have given it up.

A few miles to the west, one of America's most famous writers, Louis Bromfield, has purchased several old farms and put them together as a model of sustainable agriculture. He calls the combined operation Malabar Farm, and he becomes an ardent advocate for farming in a way that protects the land and its productivity. Malabar is made famous by Bromfield's books and by the marriage and honeymoon of the farm's most famous guests—film stars Humphrey Bogart and Lauren Bacall—in 1945. In time, Malabar will become another state park and tourism draw for the area.

Unlike so many of America's agricultural communities, Loudonville will survive thanks in part to outsiders. Over the next 60 years, the village's population count in the 10-year federal census will never drop below what it is 1949—2,500 souls.

The key to Loudonville area's future is its picturesque river—various branches of the Mohican, carving their sinuous way through the hills to enter the Walhonding, which in turn joins the Tuscarawas to form the Muskingham en route to the Ohio, the Mississippi, and the Gulf of Mexico.

Loudonville will become known as the heart of "Mohican Country," attracting recreationists of all sorts—campers, hikers, boaters, equestrians, sightseers, and especially canoeists. Within two decades, canoe liveries along the Mohican will spread Loudonville's name across Ohio, attracting outdoor adventurers from the state's big and small cities.

The community will have more than the river to thank. To Loudonville's good fortune, the Ohio Department of Natural Resources began purchasing eroded, abandoned hillside and hilltop farm land in 1928, creating the Mohican-Memorial State Forest. And during the Great Depression, Franklin D.

Roosevelt's Civilian Conservation Corps replanted these hills with native forest species—two million trees—and built roads, bridges and fire watch towers.

And at almost exactly the same time when Hortense and George and their new family arrive back into town to re-establish roots in Loudonville, the State of Ohio establishes Mohican State Park just outside town.

The state forest and state park adjoin Pleasant Hill Lake, a reservoir created by the U.S. Army Corps of Engineers in the 1940s by damming the Clear Fork of the Mohican River. The reservoir, set among the forest-covered hills, will become a haven for boaters, campers and, eventually, civilized lodge patrons.

Meanwhile, local people are starting to think Loudonville should have its own hospital so people don't always have to travel to Mansfield or other cities for medical care. Before the next decade has passed into the history books, they will make it so, and they will name it Kettering-Mohican, honoring the river and one of the local Indian tribes as well as the village's prodigy—Charles Kettering, inventor of the electric cash register, automobile self-starter, four-wheel brakes and 140 or so other patented wonders of engineering.

Yes, in 1949, change is in the air—the good, clean country air of this village established in 1814.

Few families will experience more change, more suddenly, than the Workmans and Laswells of Loudonville.

By now, Ralph Workman Sr.'s Workman Guernsey Dairy is history, and he and his new wife, Marie, are living on a small hillside farm just north of town, raising some cattle and breeding and showing boxer dogs, which have become a very popular, even glamorous, breed in America.

Although Ralph Sr. has long since gone out of the dairy business, the old family farm on East Main Street at the edge of town still has a large sign, visible for miles: "Workman Guernsey Dairy."

However, the East Main Street farm, at this point in time, is not owned by Ralph Sr. His mother, Viola Stacher

Workman, willed it to her three beloved grandsons Junior, Gene and Jack at her death in 1946.

Hortense's plan in returning to Loudonville is to move her family to the old farm as soon as the current tenant's lease is up in the coming fall of 1949. Because the farm is held in trust for her three oldest sons, living there will be more affordable and homey for the family. In the meantime, they will live in a two-story rented house in town at 440 North Wood Street.

When the farm lease is up, Hortense, George, Gene and Jack haul their belongings—and little Davy—down the hill on North Wood Street and then left on East Main, up the hill to the edge of town, just across the invisible line into Holmes County, to the farm built by David and Rebecca Stacher—Viola Workman's parents—around 1880.

The graceful old farm house commands a view of the countryside. Its front faces Route 39, the road leading east to the village of Nashville and on to Millersburg, the Holmes County seat.

The back porch looks out over the valley of the Mohican River and over Route 3 heading northeast to Wooster. A hawk soaring above just might see the farms to the north and east where the Workmans settled a century earlier after arriving from Jelloway.

On one of those early Workman farms, right next to Route 3, stands a one-room log cabin in remarkably good condition. It was built by Morgan Workman and his first wife, Jerutia Priest Workman, about 1840. In time for Loudonville's sesquicentennial celebration year of 1964, that Workman cabin will be disassembled, moved and rebuilt in Loudonville's Central Park as a lasting testimonial to all of the area's early settlers.

In the decades that will follow, children and grandchildren and great-grandchildren of Hortense and Ralph Workman Sr. and George Laswell will visit the cabin in Central Park many times, making photos and marveling at their family origins in this valley.

However, it is the East Main Street farm that will become a living memory to Hortense's children and grandchildren. They will experience it, live it, breathe it, even dream about it.

In the fall of 1949, the house consists of two tall stories, built above an earthen-floor basement on a foundation of cut, fitted stones. Its windows are tall and narrow—about the size of a grown man. The roof is covered with tin, with lightning rods poised at each end to direct any lightning strikes from the frequent Ohio summer storms safely into the ground.

At the rear, north side of the house is a summer kitchen. In the days before electric stoves when cooking was done on wood burning stoves, cooking inside the farm house on hot, muggy summer days would turn the interior of the house into a sauna. Life in the house was more tolerable if hot-weather cooking was done in the summer kitchen.

Road access to the house and farm is via a U-shaped lane off Route 39—East Main Street. The lane passes the east side of the house, where visitors get out of their vehicles and follow the walkway to the small, gingerbread-fringed front porch. Past the house, the lane continues around the rear of the home before dropping westward towards the two-story barn, then curving back to Route 39. Thus, it is possible to enter the old farm off the main road, then return to the road without ever turning your car or tractor—or, in the old days, your buggy or sleigh—around.

Between the house and the barn, the lane passes a round metal corn crib and a small, square milk house where cans of milk fresh from the cows are temporarily stored in the relative cool of the sunken building.

The barn is of a type known as the Ohio Bank Barn. At ground level, there are stalls where the cattle and other livestock—sometimes pigs, sometimes sheep—come in out of the weather. The ground level is visible from three sides, and has an entrance from the U-shaped lane.

At the back side of the barn, an earthen ramp, or bank, leads up to the second level, where sliding doors can be opened and shut. Inside the second level, farm equipment and hay for the livestock can be stored.

In the floor between the two levels is a trap door, allowing hay to be dropped down to the animal stalls below.

By the time Hortense, George and the three boys move into the big farmhouse, they have more big news. Another baby will be joining them next spring. Hortense's fifth, and Hortense's and George's second, child is on the way!

Life is anything but easy for this growing family.

Hortense—a busy mother with two older sons at home, an infant son, and a baby on the way—finds work at Loudonville's Red & White Grocery. One of the regular customers there, who will long remember Hortense, is Esther Shearer.

Esther, who is destined to become Gene's mother-in-law, will remember Hortense as a sweet and lovely person. Hortense must also be an exhausted woman.

On at least one occasion during her fifth pregnancy, Hortense visits Huffman relatives at one of the old homesteads east of Loudonville, and gets permission to gather potatoes from the field by the river. Years later, cousin Evelyn will sadly remember the sight of her pregnant cousin bent over in the back-breaking work of picking the tubers.

In 1949, George has a job of some sort in Loudonville, although the family memory of it passes into eternity with the deaths of Ralph Jr., Gene and Jack Workman in 1996, 2001 and 2006, respectively.

George Laswell, who is neither farmer nor merchant nor skilled tradesman, is gaining a reputation among Hortense's relatives and other people around Loudonville. It's not a reputation to write home about.

Hortense herself is running out of patience.

Sometime during this time, Hortense decides it is time for a portrait of her youngest son. She dresses Davy up in a cute little bib-overall outfit, shirt and two-tone shoes. Judging from the skillful hand stitching, it appears that the pants have been made especially for Davy. Hortense parts his blond hair just so, and he cooperates by sitting up straight and making a little grin. He has the look of a boy who is loved, and knows it.

March 23, 1950, dawns in the Loudonville area.

Local people who buy the Mansfield newspaper learn that their phone rates will be going up 19 percent. The other story topping the paper today is about Senator Joseph McCarthy of Wisconsin, who will go down in history for his demagoguery and for political witch hunts that destroy countless lives and careers. On this day, the Senator is attacking President Truman for refusing to cooperate with his investigation of public servants' "loyalty." Only later will CBS newsman Edward R. Murrow become a national hero for risking his career and calling the senator out on the new medium of national TV.

On the positive side, today's paper announces that 23,406 citizens of Mansfield area are registered to vote in the upcoming primary election on May 2, and hordes of basketball fans will be turning out tonight for a big pep rally to cheer on the Mansfield High School Tygers before the local hoopsters head to Columbus to compete in the state basketball championship against the Springfield High School Wildcats.

In Loudonville, 17-year-old Gene and 13-year-old Jack head off to school. The time has come for Hortense's cookie-baking date with Aunt Grace. She gets into the car and makes 23-mile trip down Route 3 to Mount Vernon.

Sometime during the day of March 23, something goes terribly wrong.

Hortense is rushed to Mercy Hospital in Mount Vernon, Ohio, to the emergency room. She has suffered a heart attack. In the afternoon, undoubtedly fearing for Hortense's well-being, the doctors induce the baby. And thus is born Cynthia Jo Laswell.

For those who will love Cynthia during her all-too-short time on this earth, her birth is the very best thing about March 23, 1950. She will light up so many lives, and create so many happy memories, for her friends and family during her 21 years.

In the hospital, Hortense is desperately weak and fragile from the heart attack and the childbirth. She wants one thing. After four sons, one of them still in diapers, Hortense has a little girl to hold in her arms and in her heart.

She asks to see her new baby girl. The doctor says no, she needs a night's rest. "Tomorrow morning, you can see her," the doctor says. Tomorrow morning.

Early in the morning, Hortense asks again to see little Cynthia. "Not now," a nurse says. "We're going to feed her. You go ahead and eat breakfast." Before little Cynthia is brought into her mother's room, Hortense suffers another heart attack. This one is fatal.

Thirty-four years later, on a summer drive around Loudonville and all the old home places, Gene Workman will remember with great sadness: "Mother never got to hold Cynthia."

And Cynthia never knew the sweet intimacy of being held in her mother's arms, and drawn to her mother's breast. Not on this earth. The heartbreak will echo through the generations of Hortense's family.

One March 24, 1950, Gene and Jack awake on the farm in Loudonville. Undoubtedly, worry about their mother occupies their minds.

Ralph Jr. is in Philadelphia on this morning. By now, he is driving trucks across America for a living. Junior's home base is Springfield. This morning, however, he is in the City of Brotherly Love, 450 road miles east of Loudonville.

Before heading off to high school, Gene is down in the barn doing the chores. There are always chores on the farm. Livestock to be fed. Milking to be done. Animal dirt to be removed.

While he is in the barn, the awful news comes from Mount Vernon. The news upends Gene's life. It could break a weaker person. In fact, it likely DOES break a weaker person, but that person is not Gene Workman.

The next day's newspaper from nearby Mansfield tells the story of the family's tragedy: Mrs. Hortense M. Laswell, 43, of East Main Street, Loudonville, says the Mansfield News-Journal, "died at 7 a.m. today of a heart attack in Mercy Hospital at Mount Vernon after a heart attack yesterday and giving birth to a daughter."

When Pastor Lester Dresch conducts her funeral service three days later at Trinity Evangelical and Reformed Church in Loudonville, one of those attending is Harold Obrecht, who had been her high school classmate and friend. It is a sign of his respect and admiration and liking for her. Forty-seven years later, Harold will recall that day for Hortense's youngest son.

One person who never knows Hortense, at least on this earth, is her only daughter, Cynthia. Such a beautiful name for a beautiful and precious child. In time, her name will be given to other beautiful and precious children in her extended family.

Cynthia, the history books recount, is the name associated with the twin sister of the ancient god of Greek mythology—Apollo. But how does Cynthia Laswell come to have this name? The answer will reveal itself one day, but not for a very long time.

For now, the newborn girl must survive—and thrive, if possible—an infancy and childhood without the mother who desperately wanted to hold her, the mother who loved her and yearned to look deeply into her eyes and to give her a good life.

Now, it will fall to others to give Cynthia and her infant brother, Davy, life and love and care.

Who will do this?

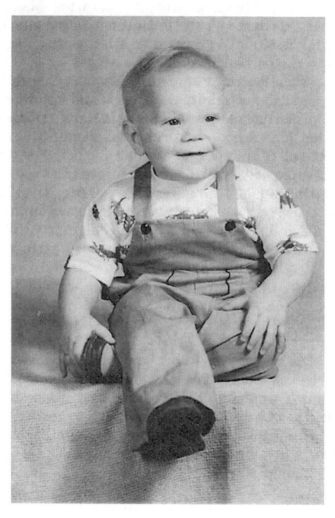

A happy David in his first year

—6—
Whose Children Are These?

Suddenly, George Laswell is a single parent with two tiny children and two teenage stepsons living in his household and depending on him. Unfortunately, it soon becomes apparent that George is not up to the job. He will not be the one who holds the family together.

This job will fall to Gene Workman, who is in his junior year at Loudonville High School.

George will disappear from the farm for unpredictable periods of time.

Seventeen-year-old Gene demonstrates the courage, determination and strength of character that will distinguish him all the rest of his life.

While he is at school or doing the farm chores, the cooking and child care fall to Rhea Stouffer, the Loudonville woman who has been a fixture in the family for years.

Rhea has long been Hortense's friend and paid helper. Now, Gene manages to scrape together the money to pay Rhea, who for a time will be the closest thing that Hortense's children have to a mom.

With Rhea's help, Gene makes sure Cynthia and Davy have a home, care and feeding, and love. During the second year of David's life, a photo is taken in front of the farm house. Gene and Rhea pose with a chubby little Davy, who is standing with his head turned just so with Gene's hand touching the little brother's ear. A strikingly handsome Gene is standing slightly behind Rhea, who is wearing her apron and a house dress. Davy looks very safe and contented in this place with these people.

On Sunday morning, June 11, 1950, Gene and Rhea make sure the two infants are dressed appropriately for the short drive into town to the Trinity Evangelical and Reformed Church, where generations of Hortense's family members have worshiped, attended Sunday School, and celebrated the full circle of life—baptism and confirmation into the Christian faith, marriages, and funerals. On any Sunday, this church is full of relatives of Hortense.

This morning, it will be recorded that David Lee Laswell and Cynthia Jo Laswell are "Baptized into the Name of the Father, and of the Son, and of the Holy Spirit" by Pastor Lester Dresch.

The children's baptismal sponsors are Miss Edna Beck and Mr. Clarence Beck. Whether George Laswell, the father, is present is not recorded.

Decades later, David will learn that Edna and Clarence were an unmarried sister and brother who are shirt-tail relatives of Hortense's family. Edna takes a personal interest in the children of the church.

Thirty five or so years after this baptismal day, David will be traveling through Loudonville area to visit brother Gene and family, and he will stop at a pay phone and call Pastor Dresch and thank him for bringing him into the body of Christ and Christian faith.

The pastor, surprised by the call, will easily remember Hortense and having loaned her the Dresch family's baby carriage after her return to Loudonville. For David, the conversation satisfies a deep need to thank the people who have touched his life in uplifting, lifesaving ways.

In the fall of 1950, Gene begins his senior year of high school. His days consist of studying, attending classes, practicing and playing football for the Redbirds, looking after David and Cynthia, and working the farm to help make ends meet. Jack, 14 years old and entering eighth grade, has his share of chores as well.

Thanksgiving of 1950 is one that Gene, Jack and millions more people in the eastern half of the United States will remember, and tell stories about, for a long, long time.

On November 23, the snow begins to fall in northeast Ohio. When it stops, it will be known variously as "The Blizzard of 1950," the "Thanksgiving Storm of 1950," and the "Great Appalachian Storm of 1950."

Hurricane-force winds form initially in North Carolina while another storm weakens over the Great Lakes. The convergence of these events sends hurricane winds barreling into New England.

The storm sweeps through 22 states, kills 353 people, and knocks out power to a million customers. It injures more than 160 more.[xii]

One event that is not interrupted is the annual football clash between the Ohio State University Buckeyes and the University of Michigan Wolverines. Their game in the Buckeyes' stadium will be immediately dubbed the Snow Bowl. Sadly for Ohioans, the Wolverines win the epic contest. The Buckeyes will have to get even in years to come. At many of those future games, Gene and Mickey Workman and their children and grandchildren will be in the stands, cheering on their Ohio State football team.

In some areas of Ohio, the storm unloads about two feet of snow. In Springfield, it's deep enough that newspaper delivery boy Dan Quinn's canvas delivery bag drags through the snow, leaving a trail as he walks his route. In Loudonville, it dumps a foot or more, disrupting motorized travel on streets and roads. In the 21st century, it's easy to underestimate the power of a blizzard to shut things down in 1950.

In the middle of the 20th century, most four-wheel drive vehicles are known as Willys Jeeps, and most of them belong to the United States military. American passenger cars and pickup trucks have front engines and rear-wheel drive, which means the weight of the engine does nothing to improve traction; to the contrary, the drive wheels are forced to push against the weight of the engine, causing many a spinout on a snowy or icy road.

In 1950, most cars have a three-speed stick shift on the steering column, although automatic transmissions in the form of the General Motors Hydra-Matic are beginning to gain popularity.

Tire technology isn't much help in a snow storm, either. Steel-belted radial tires are not yet known on American roadways, having just been introduced in Europe by Michelin. Studded snow tires are unheard of.

And so it is that, when the Blizzard of 1950 buries Loudonville, 17-year-old Gene Workman needs to figure out how best to get from the hilltop farm on East Main Street into town for groceries and supplies—and then get back up the hill.

As it so happens, there is an old one-horse open sleigh in the barn. When it was last used, and by whom, is anybody's guess.

There is also a horse on the place. It's possible that Gene is boarding it in return for a little income for the family. The horse does have one issue, which will reveal itself soon enough.

Now, Gene has to find harness to attach the horse to the sleigh, or vice versa, depending on your point of view. Gene borrows it from a cousin on a nearby farm. How he retrieves it is not one of the details that he will pass on in the telling of the story.

At any rate, when the time comes, Gene harnesses the horse, climbs into the sleigh with little Davy, snaps the reigns, and heads the outfit down into town. This is where the issue with the horse comes in.

The horse is moon-eyed, meaning it has lost sight in one eye. As a result, the animal will only allow itself to turn the sleigh in the direction of the good eye. In order to make turn in the opposite direction, Gene must follow the horse's lead, making a complete circuit around the block, in the direction of the good eye, until the horse can see the intended destination.

Telling the story in 1984, Gene recalls turning into the U-lane back at the farm. As the sleigh makes the turn, too fast, little bundled-up Davy rolls out into a pile of snow. Gene laughs in the retelling. "I dumped you right here in this driveway."

Brother David will forever after have a new appreciation when singing "Jingle Bells" and when reading Lydia Maria Child's early American Thanksgiving poem, which begins:

> *Over the river and through the wood,*
> *To Grandmother's house we go;*

The horse knows the way to carry the sleigh
Through the white and drifted snow. [xiii]

David will later learn, from an older cousin, that people all around town are paying attention to 17-year-old Gene and how he handles himself, his younger siblings, and takes whatever life throws at him. Whether Gene knows it or not, many eyes are on him, and he will continue to impress people all of his life.

By all accounts, George Laswell—father of the two infant children—isn't any help to Gene. George comes, he goes, and he wants to be in charge when he shows up. Sometimes with a woman.

Finally, Gene confronts his stepfather: "George, these are your kids (referring to Davy and Cynthia). If you want to raise them, then do it. But you can't keep coming and going. Be the father."

Meanwhile, an ocean away across the International Dateline, a conflict is under way that will take boys and men from farms, small towns and big cities across America. In sending troops to try to defeat the Communist-allied troops in northern Korea, President Truman calls it "a police action" and the Korean Conflict. Later generations will know it for what it is: the Korean War.

In three years, from 1950 to 1953, five million civilians and soldiers from many nations will lose their lives in a war that is destined to haunt Americans in the second decade of the 21st century. [xiv]

When Gene turns 18 in 1951, near the end of his senior year in high school, he is required by law to register for the military draft. His place of registration is Millersburg, the government seat for Holmes County. This is because the Workman / Stacher farm is just inside the Holmes County boundary.

Gene is number 18 on the induction list. In a county with a large Amish population, which ardently believes in pacifism, 12 of the young men listed ahead of him are designated

Conscientious Objectors. This means the United States will not draft them into the military.

Gene wonders whether he can get a crop in this year to make some income for his brothers and sister. A draft board official tells him: "If I were you, I would plan on being around to plant the corn this spring, but I would not plan on being around to harvest it."

Gene enlists in the Navy, taking himself off the draft list. This means he will serve a minimum of four years in the military, but he will not be lugging a rifle around the mountains of Korea.

In the summer, after his graduation from Loudonville High School, Gene leaves for Basic Training, courtesy of Uncle Sam. He will spend the next four years as a machinist's mate assigned to the cruiser USS Helena. This Loudonville farm boy will spend a large amount of those four years in the Helena's engine room—two years in the combat zone along the coast of the Korean peninsula.

When Gene leaves, George is suddenly, solely responsible for his two-year-old son and one-year-old daughter.

Fourteen-year-old Jack moves in with his father, Ralph Workman Sr., and stepmother Marie, who are living on a small farm north of town.

George makes the decision to go back to Dayton with his children. Maybe he expects to find work there. Rhea, now the family mainstay, agrees to go with him to take care of the children.

Sometime during these months, George Laswell poses for a snapshot with his two little towheaded children. They are on the stoop of a very modest-looking home. George is crouching, with his arms around the tikes, who are standing in front. George looks like he might be a happy dad. David is looking at George and Cynthia; tiny, diapered Cynthia looks rather bewildered.

If George is a happy family man, it doesn't last long.

In October 1951, Rhea gets into a car in Dayton, or perhaps takes the bus, and makes the trip home to Loudonville with 17-month-old Cynthia, to attend the village's big annual event—the Loudonville Street Fair. Sixty-three years later, the organizers of this event will sum up in four words what the town Street Fair is all about.

"Small Town, Big Fair" the event website will declare. Then, elaborating:

> *Our small town hosts a big fair that is truly an old-fashioned, family-oriented event in downtown Loudonville, Ohio. We offer five days of free admission, free entertainment, free exhibits, free livestock shows and auctions, free power pulls, rides, food and more. The Loudonville Street Fair begins each day at 12 noon and runs until 10:00 p.m. each night from September 30—October 4, 2014. State routes 3 and 60 are closed during the event. Our small town hosts a big fair that is truly an old-fashioned, family-oriented event in downtown Loudonville, Ohio. Tents, rides, games, exhibits. A lot like a county fair, only everything takes place on city streets.*

It's not an exaggeration. People from miles around come to the Street Fair. In 1951, Rhea heads northeast with little Cynthia.

George stays behind with 2½-year-old David. He loses little time getting the heck out of Dodge.

Soon after Rhea and Cynthia leave the house on Meeker Road in Dayton, George packs a few items into a delivery truck belonging to his employer. He climbs in with David, and off they go.

George will never again lay eyes, or arms, on his daughter.

David and Cynthia, the little brother and sister who so closely resemble one another, will never again live together as members of the same household.

In these days of 1951, before every family has at least one television, and before the Internet has even been imagined, information passes slowly.   A father and son can seem to disappear into thin air. And that is exactly what George Laswell and little David do.

No one except George knows where he and little David go next. Even in a stolen truck, there's no way to find them, although people will try hard. Days pass with no word about the father and son. Weeks pass. Months pass. No member of Hortense's family knows a thing. Little David and his father have simply, achingly vanished.

Gene, Rhea and David at the
Workman / Stacher Farm

Only known photo of George with
David and Cynthia

Gene Workman, USS Helena, 1951–55

—7—
A New Family, and a Search

When Machinist's Mate Gene Workman hears about Davy's disappearance and Cynthia's return to Loudonville with Rhea, he is in no position to do anything about it.

First, he belongs to the United States Navy, and a fighting war is on. Second, he is sick and assigned to the infirmary at the Navy base in San Diego.

Rhea will remain in Loudonville and move in with her brother-in-law, the widower of her late sister. Cynthia will remain with her. For all practical purposes, Rhea has become the mother, and will never willingly give her up. Each month, Gene sends money from his Navy pay to help provide for his little sister. He also makes sure that Rhea receives money for Cynthia from Hortense's Social Security survivor's benefit.

Cynthia and her new family live in the upstairs apartment of a two-story house on South Water Street that is heated in winter by steam radiators in each room. Behind the house is an alley where, in times past, horses and carriages were ridden to and from their in-town barns. Beyond the alley is a riverside park along the Clear Fork of the Mohican River.

Meanwhile, the news of Davy's disappearance sends a shock wave through his oldest brother, Ralph Jr., who is living a few miles from Dayton in Springfield.

Ralph Jr. came to Springfield in the mid-1940s while working for Walgreen's, America's Midwestern chain of pharmacy stores. His job was working the soda fountains and lunch counters.

Sometime after arriving here, he landed a job driving for a company that delivers International Harvester truck cabs all across the country. This job made him member of the International Brotherhood of Teamsters. It's good work, and

53 |

pays very well in these postwar years when America is the economic engine for the world.

The one drawback is that he is gone on the road for days on end.

In 1951, Springfield is a thriving industrial town of about 78,000 souls, surrounded by rich, mostly flat farmland that produces bumper yields of corn, tomatoes, strawberries, pumpkins, squash, poultry, cattle, swine. The city, built along the old National Road (U.S. 40) is also home to a lot of manufacturing. Whatever America needs, towns like Springfield in the Middle West build it.

After arriving in Springfield, Ralph marries a young woman he loves, who has an infant daughter.

Ralph buys a home at the corner of Beatrice Street and Champion Avenue. For mid-20th century Midwestern America, it's a cute little place, something of a bungalow, with three bedrooms, an unfinished basement, and a modern natural gas furnace.

And then one day, Ralph returns from a road trip of several days. In the basement, he finds his young wife's lifeless body. While the investigation will find there was no foul play, that fact will be no comfort to her loved ones. The memory of that awful moment will forever haunt the young man. Ralph's grief-stricken in-laws gain custody of their granddaughter, and they make it very clear that he is no longer their son-in-law or the stepfather of their granddaughter.

Eventually, time begins its healing therapy, and Ralph Workman is introduced to a fun-loving, attractive—and resilient—woman named Louise, who is visiting her sister's family across the street from Ralph's home.

Louise's sister Katie and her husband, Ernie Muse, play the role of match-makers. It's the same Ernie Muse who, a few years ago, was operating a dozer and shooting rattlers for the expansion of Wright Field. Although Louise lives in Nashville, Tennessee, she and Ralph see more and more of each other.

They will be a darling couple with loads of friends.

Louise is trim, nicely dressed without a hint of extravagance, and well-schooled by her Southern parents in proper manners and social graces. Her brunette hair is full-bodied with curls. Her dark eyes sparkle with vitality.

Ralph is tall and, in his 20s and 30s, lives up to his childhood nickname of "Slim." He has jet-black hair and radiant blue-gray eyes. His easy-going personality belies a quiet power and strength that only rarely reveals itself. His children will come to realize that Ralph Workman Jr. is not a man to be bullied, threatened or otherwise messed with.

Louise has two children—smart, witty, great-looking kids with the reddest hair in town (two towns, really—one in Ohio and one in Tennessee). Danny and Peggy Welch, and their mom, have had their share of heartache. The father, Courtney, died in a horrible industrial accident at a chemical plant in their home state of Tennessee during the war, before his children could know him.

Louise has had steady work as a Bell Telephone operator, in a time when calls are routed via wires into switchboards, where a real-live human-being (usually female) operator would put your call through to its destination. Life as a widow with children has been a struggle, but Louise has managed to make ends meet.

In 1951, Ralph and Louise get into the car and drive west to Indiana, an hour away, to make their marriage vows. Then they return to Springfield on U.S. 40.

Once again, Ralph Workman Jr. has a family, and he begins, slowly and steadily, to win the hearts of Peggy and Danny.

Louise gets a job at the Crowell-Collier Publishing Company in downtown Springfield—a sprawling magazine printing plant that occupies an entire city block. In this building are printed several of America's most popular magazines, such as *Collier's*, *Woman's Home Companion*, and *The Country Home*. The printing plant is enormous, including seven buildings and covering 20 acres of floor space.[xv]

Shortly before they begin their new lives together in the little home on Beatrice Street, Ralph receives the news of little David's disappearance.

Two of Ralph's enduring qualities manifest themselves. One of them is his big heart—big as all outdoors, Peggy will later say. Ralph Workman Jr. is a man who cares. Another quality is his strength of character and of purpose. At six feet, four inches tall, Ralph Workman is not a man to shrug his shoulders and let things slide. When something is wrong, he will try to set it right.

And now, he is determined to find his missing brother— Hortense's youngest son. In this, Ralph is joined by Louise. They will spare nothing to find Davy. Peggy and Danny support this decision. A new family, just learning to be a unit, has resolved to do this together.

It is immaterial to Ralph, Louise, Danny and Peggy that David has been taken away by the man who is listed on the birth certificate as the father. What kind of man, they ask, would disappear with his son and abandon his daughter?

But where to start to find a missing two-year-old?

In 1951, before there is such a thing as "America's Most Wanted" television programming or an Amber Alert missing-child notification, how does one go about tracking down a missing person?

Ralph notifies the police. It's also likely that George's former employer reports the theft of the company delivery truck.

Ralph and Louise hire private detectives and place ads in several newspapers. In these days, it is the best hope they have. Newspapers and word of mouth are the primary ways that people get information about their communities.

The question is, will the "private eyes" and advertisements buried deep in a few newspapers find a little boy and his father, who could be anywhere?

Louise became the perfect
match for Ralph

Ralph won the hearts of
Dan and Peggy

Louise, top right, and a friend with Peggy and Dan

—8—
A Startling Letter, and a Phone Call

In May 1952, in a house in rural Alabama outside the port city of Mobile, Luella Smith, a widow with several children, sits down at her table, picks up a pen or pencil, straightens a piece of paper, and begins to write a letter.

It is addressed to complete strangers nearly 700 miles away.

> *"Dear Friend,"* she writes.
>
> *"I am writing you to ask you to please do me a favor.*
>
> *"Late November or early December a Mr. George S. Laswell from 8400 Meeke(r) Road, Dayton, came to Mobile with his little son, David, whom the doctors said could not live north because of his health. Since I have had him he has gained weight, and is a happy little boy who loves us, and whom we all love.*
>
> *"At first the father called almost daily and then I didn't hear from him for some weeks. He called, saying he had almost died. Since then, I have not heard from him, and am wondering if he is ill, or what has happened.*
>
> *"Perhaps someone there in Dayton could give me some light on this, as we are quite worried and want to know, and be able to tell him, where the boy's father is."*
>
> *Mrs. Carl G. Smith*
> *Route 2, Box 80-E, Mobile, Alabama.*

Where to send it? How to address the envelope?

Luella hopes it will be published in a newspaper in the town where George Laswell last lived. How would she know which newspaper in Dayton to send it to? Does she address the envelope "Newspaper, Dayton, Ohio"?

The odds are against her, and against the little boy who is in her charge.

In a sizable city like Dayton, Ohio, a newspaper in 1952 gets a lot of mail. Even if Luella's letter arrives at a newspaper office, where will it be routed? Where will it land?

Will anybody notice? Will anybody care?

The Dayton Daily News and the Journal Herald in 1952 are two newspapers produced by the same company—Cox Newspapers. The Daily News is published in the afternoon; the Journal Herald (known by some as "The JH") is published in the morning.

The people who run the presses, the people who set the lead type, the people who sell advertising and subscriptions, the people who get tens of thousands of fat newspapers delivered to porches all over the Miami Valley of Ohio . . . they all do their work for the same company.

The people who collect the money, who count the money, who pay the bills, who distribute the mail, all do these jobs for the same company.

However, the people who fill the newspaper with words and pictures do not work for both papers. These people—called "editorial staff" or "journalists"—work either for the Daily News or for the Journal Herald in 1952. Although they are paid by the same newspaper corporation, they are competitors when it comes to creating an informative, interesting, newsy newspaper that people will read and talk about.

James Cox Sr., who built this newspaper company and added the Journal Herald in 1948-49 through the purchase and merger of two earlier morning papers, wants it this way. He wants his readers—all of them—to get their money's worth, and to keep subscribing to the newspaper that they like best. He caters to the customers' interests and likes and habits.

So if Mrs. Carl G. Smith's letter does arrive at the right Dayton newspaper building, what will happen to it? Where might it land among the dozens of "editorial" staff / journalists who get newspapers out every single day?

And if someone at one of the newspapers reads her letter, what will this person think? It could be considered "too personal." If lawyers are consulted, they might counsel restraint. After all, there are people named in the letter. Real people, supposedly. What if the letter isn't accurate? What if somebody gets an idea to sue for damages?

As it turns out, Luella Smith's letter lands in exactly the right place. It goes to the Journal Herald into the internal mail slot for Chesta Fulmer.

Chesta Fulmer, in 1952, is the "Ann Landers" or "Dear Abby" of Dayton. She writes an advice column in the Journal Herald, called "We Together." People write to her, and she writes back, right there on the pages of the morning newspaper.

In mid-20th century, many Daytonians start their day reading Chesta. Four decades later, another Dayton journalist will declare that Chesta "developed a following that was near idolatry."[xvi] In 1957, when Chesta Fulmer dies, her obituary is published in newspapers far away from Dayton, Ohio.

In early May 1952, Chesta reads the letter from an unknown woman in Mobile, Alabama.

On May 16, in her "We Together" column, Chesta publishes Luella Smith's letter. It's on Page 31, in the Journal Herald's *Modern Living* section, which trumpets "News For And About Today's Women," including "Fashions—Fine Arts— Frills."

Luella's letter is the third and final item in the May 16 column. The headline is: "LETTER FROM ALABAMA."

The letter occupies three and three-quarters vertical inches and four and one-eighth horizontal inches of newspaper space.

The letter, as published, includes George's fabrication about David's health being too frail to survive the heated premises of houses built in Dayton, Ohio, which at this time in history is one of the most prosperous places on earth.

At the end of Luella's letter, Chesta prints her only comment:

"Dear Friend: I am sure anyone knowing this gentleman will contact you. Perhaps he is ill somewhere. I can well understand your worry, and hope that you get good news."

That's it. That's all there is.

It is enough.

Somewhere in the Dayton area, one of Chesta Fulmer's thousands of faithful readers is surely shocked by these words printed in the morning paper.

Somehow this anonymous person has made it past the headlines, the big news of the day on the front page of the paper—stories such as the political squabbling between President Harry Truman and Thomas Dewey, who had lost the 1948 election to Truman; such as a big labor settlement by two of the nation's big oil companies; such as a report that America's deadly atomic weapons strategy will be reviewed by military officials of the Supreme Headquarters Allied Powers Europe, headed by General Dwight Eisenhower.

He or she, most likely she, makes it past the article on the *Modern Living* page in which Mrs. Dwight Eisenhower grants an interview describing how much she will miss France, now that she and Ike are leaving Europe. The United Press dispatch from Paris describes Mrs. Eisenhower buying a $12.50 suitcase to bring home souvenirs.

The anonymous reader also makes it through the first two items in Chesta's "We Together" column—first, the introduction where Chesta expresses her personal conviction that anger and "getting even" are self-defeating; and then the second item, titled "Teenage Rebellion."

Finally, the anonymous reader's eye is caught by the last item of today's "We Together" column, the one headlined "Letter from Alabama."

This person knows of George Laswell, and knew Hortense. Perhaps Hortense and this anonymous newspaper reader worked together at Frigidaire. Perhaps they were neighbors or friends. Whoever this person is, she or he gets on the phone and contacts Ralph Workman Sr.

And this phone call sets off a breathtaking chain of events that will reverberate far into the future in the Workman family.

Kindness shows in this photo of a young Luella

★

LETTER FROM ALABAMA

Dear Friend:

I am writing asking you to please do me a favor.

Late November or early December a Mr. George S. Laswell from 8400 Meeke road, Dayton, came to Mobile with his little son, whom the doctors said could not live north because of his health. Since I have had him he has gained weight, and is a happy little boy who loves us, and whom we all love.

At first the father called almost daily and then I didn't hear from him for some weeks. He called, saying he had almost died. Since then I have not heard from him, and am wondering if he is ill, or what has happened.

Perhaps someone there in Dayton could give me some light on this, as we are quite worried and want to know, and be able to tell him, where the boy's father is.

> MRS. CARL G. SMITH,
> Route 2, Box 80-E,
> Mobile, Ala.

Dear Friend:

I am sure anyone knowing this gentleman will contact you. Perhaps he is ill somewhere. I can well understand your worry, and hope that you get good news.

The Dayton Journal Herald on May 16, 1952

—9—
The Trip South

In the little house on Beatrice Street, there is jubilation. Ralph Jr. gets his hands on a copy of the Dayton Journal Herald and neatly clips out the Letter from Alabama—a document that, in the Workman family, will become as important as a birth certificate. On the back, he writes the date—"5-16-52"—and he initials it: "RW".

Junior quickly lines up a way to get himself from the heartland of Ohio to the Gulf Coast of Dixie, and back.

At Howard Sober Trucking, where he now works, he arranges to be the driver who makes the next delivery of International Harvester trucks to Mobile, Alabama.

But this trip is no cakewalk. One aspect of Ralph Workman Jr.'s makeup is his ability to anticipate what might go wrong. He imagines the possibilities when he, an outsider, shows up in Alabama and leaves the state—then crosses several state lines—with three-year-old David Laswell, who is not his son. This tall, lanky Ohioan does not want to trigger suspicion as he ventures about the Deep South.

From Springfield, he gets on the phone and places a call to Alabama, speaking to Mrs. Carl G. Smith.

The call must come as a relief to Luella. Finally, someone cares enough about the boy to inquire about him. On the phone, they make arrangements for the older brother to retrieve the long-lost toddler. It is likely that Luella gives him directions for finding her rural home, and he undoubtedly writes the directions down in his unique, somewhat chaotic handwriting. He is certain to ask the right questions to be sure that the little boy in Mrs. Carl G. Smith Sr.'s home is his brother—Hortense's son.

Perhaps Luella asks questions to be certain that the man on the phone is who he says he is. Anyone, after all, can respond to a plea in the newspaper.

Next, Ralph waits for the truck delivery run that will change his life, his family's life, and David's life forever.

Meanwhile, in San Diego, California, U.S. Navy sailor Gene Workman pens a letter to his older brother, Ralph Jr., in Springfield. Gene calls him "Slim." Gene apologizes for not making the trip to Springfield when he recently came home on military leave to Loudonville. And he mentions that, while on the phone to their father's home, he recently heard that "little Davy" is in Alabama and that Ralph is going to get him. Gene asks Junior to write and let him know when they bring Davy home. In the meantime, he and the USS Helena will be sailing across the Pacific to Pearl Harbor.

Before Gene's letter arrives in Springfield, Ralph Jr. climbs into the cab of a semi truck, fires up the engine, and heads for Dayton, where he will connect with U.S. 48 towards Cincinnati and the Ohio River.

He will cross through Kentucky, then Tennessee, and into the flat lands of Alabama, all the way to the Gulf Coast.

Perhaps along the way, he drops off multiple brand-new truck cabs that he has hauled piggyback for delivery.

In Mobile, Ralph obtains local transportation. Perhaps he gets a taxi. In 1952, car rental companies haven't yet dominated the landscape of American travel. Rental cars are few and far between.

Soon after arriving in the coastal city, Ralph visits the child-welfare authorities. He makes absolutely certain that he will not be accused of abducting a child and illegally transporting him across state lines—multiple states, at that.

Assurances obtained, Ralph follows the directions to Luella Smith's house in the country.

Seven years before, Luella became a widow when her husband, Carl G. Smith Sr., died of a heart attack. Carl Sr. was a ship fitter at the naval shipyard at Mobile Bay. He was also a backyard farmer who, with his wife and children, raised a variety of produce and chickens.

After Carl's death, in the last year of World War II, Luella finds herself a single parent with a minor son and daughter, in addition to her three adult children.

To help make ends meet, she does child care as a nanny. Sometimes she will take the bus to the client's home and spend the week. Other times, she will take the bus back and forth for the day. The name by which she is known to many children, in fact, is "Nanny." Her grandchildren also address her with this name. This must be what little David Laswell calls her.

Luella Camp Smith, whose Alvarez ancestors settled in Mobile in the 1770s, is 55 years old when 39-year-old George Laswell from Kentucky and Ohio finds her and leaves 2½-year-old David with her.

In years to come, David will wonder: did George find Luella in this land near the Gulf of Mexico and Mobile Bay on someone's referral, because of her child-care experience? And of all the places he could have gone with young David, why did George land here, at this city a long way from his previous homes?

The answers to these questions will prove to be elusive for the son of George and Hortense Laswell. One possibility is that the Mobile area would provide job prospects to a nurseryman. All around Mobile are commercial nurseries.

As related in Luella's "Letter from Alabama" in the Dayton newspaper, George leaves his son with her in late November or early December. According to Luella's published letter, George—before vanishing once again—told her that he almost died. Is that an exaggeration or an outright lie, as David will assume for most of his adult life? Decades later, David will come across information that will cause him to wonder.

Another mystery is why George felt attached enough to his toddler son to disappear from Ohio with him, only to leave him in a strange place hundreds of miles from the boy's family. Where George is concerned, unknowns abound. And where he goes after Mobile, Alabama, nobody will know for a very long time.

Luella and Carl Smith Sr. and daughter Margaret at
their home, early 1940s

—10—
The Big Man and the Train

Whatever the reasons for Davy's circumstances, the boy will remember next to nothing about his half year in Mobile, Alabama. He turns three years old under Luella's care. In Loudonville, Cynthia turns two under Rhea Stouffer's care. It's entirely possible that Luella doesn't know when David's birthday has come and passed.

David's only recollection of this place in Alabama will be a "freeze frame" image in his deep and distant memory. In it, David is with bigger boys in tall grass or other vegetation out in the country. Later, it will seem likely that these are grandsons who, with their parents, live for a time with "Nanny" Luella in the 1½-story clapboard house built on piers.

David probably sleeps upstairs in the converted attic / loft space, which provides beds for the boys.

On May 23, 1952, Ralph Jr. makes the trip to Luella Smith's house in the country west of town. He likely rides west on Cottage Hill Road, a main route, and turns south onto East Road, then left again onto a narrow dirt track named Greenleaf Road.

The driver would have to proceed carefully because Greenleaf has formidable drainage ditches on either side. Two vehicles cannot pass each other on Luella Smith's road in 1952.

Upon arriving at the house, does the man from Ohio step up onto the screened-in front porch and knock on her door? Or does she see him coming, and meet him outside? The stranger introduces himself.

The big man and Luella talk about the boy. Then they take a piece of paper exactly four inches by six and a half inches. Luella gets a pencil and writes out the agreement they have made.

According to the "release" that she writes to Ralph Workman Jr., the Workman family will reimburse her for board and clothing beginning January 25.

Does this mean George paid her for the boy's care during December and January? Was George working somewhere in the area during that time? These are more questions that David will one day ponder.

Ralph folds the paper and puts in into his wallet or into a pocket. During the 700 miles between Mobile and Springfield, if anyone questions why he has the little boy with him, Ralph has a document of sorts to explain.

For now, Ralph Jr. takes his little brother in hand, and they leave the Smith home and head down the dirt road between the drainage ditches. Ralph is deeply relieved to have Davy in his custody. After all the months, all the waiting, all the conversations with the private detective, the little blond boy is back with his mother's family. *His* family.

Ralph's next order of business is to get David some new clothes, suitable for a northbound trip through four states. And he gets on a pay phone and calls Louise, and tells her the news. In these times, cellular phones may exist in someone's creative imagination, but nothing like them exists in the real world. Pay phones, in booths and public places, are a vital link to the rest of the world.

A short time later, little David is boarding a train with this big man who has taken him. He is undoubtedly confused and shy, and kind of scared.

Later, he will the hear the story of how, after boarding the train, he lets Ralph know that he needs to go to the potty. While he is in there, Ralph opens the door of the restroom to make sure everything is going okay in there. The little boy slams the door shut, saying in no certain terms that he has important business in progress. Years later, Ralph laughs as he tells the story.

From now on, one of David's most vivid memories of the first three years of his life will be what comes next.

David is sitting in a seat next to the big man, and clinging to his pillow. The big man talks to him, calms him, and encourages him to sleep. The sleeping part isn't happening yet.

At this moment, another man—one wearing a uniform and a hat—walks purposefully down the aisle of the rail car. This man is called the Conductor.

Ralph thinks of just the right words to get the boy to close his eyes. "If you don't go to sleep," he says, "the Conductor will take your pillow." Magic words. In no time at all, David is fast asleep, clinging to his pillow. It's the last memory he has of the railroad car.

This train ride creates in David a lifelong love for rail travel. In the future, he will enjoy some spectacular train rides— across the United States and back, through many miles of the Russian Far East, and across the Bavarian-Austrian-Swiss Alps and Alsace region of France to Paris. None of them, however, will top this first train ride.

Louise with her mother, Jessie, in Nashville

11

Going Home to New Faces, New Places

David's next lasting memory takes place in a yard. He and the big man named Ralph are standing outside a house, next to an older man who is watering from a garden hose.

Later, David will know this man as Grandpa Alley. And he will know this place as Grandpa and Grandma Alley's house on Murphy Road in Nashville, Tennessee.

This house is where one of the most important people he will ever know grew up. However, as of yet, David has no idea that she exists.

Her name is Louise. He will always know her as Mom.

She will teach him all of the most important things that he needs to know to live a good life, a happy life, a successful life. Starting with the most important thing—that he is loved. Deeply loved.

Louise and Ralph are the life-changing, life-shaping force in his personal universe.

Never again will David "not belong."

Never will he think of himself as an orphan.

From Day One, David is accepted as a member of Ralph's and Louise's family. Right along with Big Brother Danny and Big Sister Peggy, those wonderful red-heads.

Louise and Ralph make David their son. Danny and Peggy treat him as their little brother (a sometimes snotty little brother, at that). David isn't pampered (he has, after all, outgrown diapers!). He isn't spoiled. He will now begin learning what it means to live with a family and learn a family's values. And a family's rules.

It will take a lot of patience, and good humor, along with good values to shape this boy up.

David, you see, has come equipped with two traits that don't always come as a package. He is insecure. This will take time and stable family life to cure. He also has acquired quite a vocabulary for a three-year-old. In fact, Davy has quite a potty mouth. This will not take so long to fix at Louise's and Ralph's house.

David's vocabulary education begins right away.

Soon after arriving at the house on Beatrice Street, three-year-old David looks up at 6-foot-4 Ralph Workman Jr.—and calls him a Son of a B——ch.

Years later, when the story is retold, it transpires that Ralph immediately leaves the room, breaks up in laughter, and regains his composure.

Then, with a stern look on his face, Ralph returns to young David and impresses upon the little fellow that those are not words for a child to use. Ralph is very persuasive. Suffice it to say, David never uses those words in Ralph's presence again. Ever.

David's feelings of insecurity will reveal themselves in many ways.

When he first comes to the house on Beatrice Street, he does not sleep in the bed. He sleeps under it.

Shortly afterward, his cousin Dorothy, daughter of Aunt Katie and Uncle Ernie across the street, gives him a blue and white Teddy Bear. The bear is about as big as he is.

David carries the Teddy, sleeps with the Teddy, loves the Teddy to death. Over time, Teddy loses his eyes and his nose, and pulls apart at the seams, revealing the shredded newspaper stuffing. Eventually, a very dilapidated bear finds its way into the small collection of childhood possessions that will follow David into his golden years. Both of them—David and Teddy—will reach retirement age before David finally lets his oldest friend go to the Teddy Bear Hereafter.

Teddy isn't the only object that David attaches himself to.

In kindergarten in the early 1950s, children take mats to school so all the kindergarteners can take a nap each day. One day, a loud bell goes off at Warder Park Elementary School, and all the children are led outside as part of a thing called the Fire Drill.

All the children march out with their teachers. All except one. Davy Workman—that's how he is known now—runs back INTO the school. To get his sleeping pad . . .

The teacher runs after him, and sternly impresses upon him that a sleeping pad is not worth losing your life for.

David's insecurities reveal themselves in other ways.

Louise tries every kind of child care while she continues to earn an income to bring home to her family. A lady down the street tries babysitting him, but gives up. The minute that Mrs. Workman leaves the premises, little David goes into hysterics and also wets his pants. Not once. Not twice. Every day it happens.

Eventually, Louise tries a large "day care center" that takes care of several children. It occupies the ground floor of one of the many splendid old Victorian-era mansions that line Springfield's High Street. After many pants-wettings and hysterics, the operators of the center also give up on David.

A photo snapshot of this era shows a beautiful young Louise, in a pretty dress that she has worn to work this day. David is a few feet away in the photo. On the back, Louise writes to Gene at the USS Helena: "This is as far away as he will ever get from me. I had just stepped in the yard from work. Dave hangs on for fear I will go to work again."

Louise and Ralph agree that she will become a stay-at-home mom. The family budget undoubtedly suffers. David is very satisfied with the arrangement.

After a few years, the Workman family outgrows the little house on Beatrice Street, and they move to a couple of temporary rental homes until the right house becomes available for purchase.

One of these rental houses is located on East Main Street in Springfield. In 1956, Main Street is also U.S. 40—the highway that crosses a continent, bringing cars and trucks and buses from coast to coast—Atlantic City, New Jersey, to San Francisco, California.

David is seven years old when the family moves here. Some of the things he likes about living here are: watching the Mickey Mouse Club (especially Annette Funicello) on television after school each day; and building forts with the bales of straw that the road construction workers pile up along the nearby U.S. 40 bypass as it is being completed.

One thing he does not like about living here is the night when Mom and Dad go out for the evening, leaving him in the care of a teenage babysitter. Soon after Mom and Dad leave, David begins asking the babysitter when they're coming home.

"Later on," she says.

"How soon?" he asks.

"In a little while," she says.

Soon, to calm the seven-year-old down, the babysitter takes him outside, and they sit on the front steps down near the sidewalk, which is next to Main Street. David begins watching for the car containing his mom and dad. This being U.S. 40, there are a LOT of cars. He watches each one of them, hoping it's them.

"Is that them?"

No, not yet.

"There they are; that's them."

And so it goes. In due time, of course, Mom and Dad return. David gets a big hug. Hopefully, the sitter gets a big tip.

Mom and Dad never complain to David about his about his insecurity. They just keep on loving him, and letting him know they will never leave him for as long as they live.

In time, their confidence in him gives him confidence in himself.

David will ever after enjoy a close relationship with his mom and dad—threatened only by the crazy "whitewater rapids" known as The Teenage Years.

Mom teaches David respectfulness and manners. An older man is referred to as "Mr." A married woman is called

"Mrs." An older unmarried woman is called "Miss." At this time, you see, "Ms." has not been invented.

When asking for something, you always say "Please." And remember to say "Thank you."

You say "Yes, sir" or "No, sir." You say "Yes, ma'am" or "No, ma'am."

Mom teaches him how a gentleman treats a lady. Gentlemen always open a door for a girl or a woman. Gentlemen walk on the outside, toward traffic, when accompanying a woman or a girl on a walk.

Mom teaches values, summed up in just the right sayings, such as:

"If you can't say something nice, don't say anything at all." (Don't be a complainer, and don't talk about people when they're not around.)

"If you're going to do a job, do it right."

Four decades later, the effect of this complete and unconditional love will come into full focus for David.

He and his wife are at the home of another couple who are valued friends. Following a lovely meal, Bob—a psychologist who devotes his working life to patients at a state facility, says: "Dave, you're a very positive person. You are able to love yourself, aren't you?"

This comment takes David by surprise. He has never thought of such a thing. He thinks a moment, then says: "Yes, I guess you're right."

He tells Bob: "I can't think of a time when members of my family ever belittled me or put me down."

The psychologist, who has spent his life helping people deal with the anger and frustrations and demons in their lives, responds sincerely: "You are very blessed."

"Yes," David agrees. "I am."

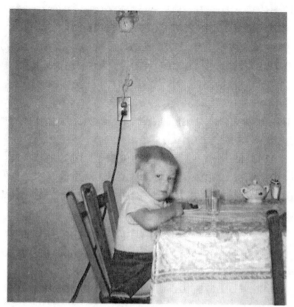

David's second week with Ralph and Louise

Louise writes on photo: "This is as far away as he
will ever get from me."

David stays close to his new brother Dan
while a friend joins in

Hangin' onto Mom on a visit to
one of the farms

12

Tale of Two Towns, and Two Families

Everyone needs a home town. It gives a person a sense of place, a sense of rootedness. Everybody needs a family. It gives a person a place of belonging and knowing.

As a Workman, David grows up with two home towns, and with a valued place in two nuclear families.

Springfield is where he lives with Ralph and Louise, and where he will acquire mentors and friends to last a lifetime. It is where many people will take a chance on him—giving him priceless opportunities. It is where so many of David's "firsts" will happen. First friends, first teachers, first job, first love, first-born daughter, first communion, and more.

One hundred and thirty road miles to the north and east, the village of Loudonville is the place of dreams and longing. It is where remarkable reconciliation happens. It is also where the sweetest girl in the world lives all through the 1950s and into the 1960s. Cynthia is her name.

David and Cynthia are the proverbial two peas in a pod. One look at them confirms that they share the same DNA. They share their blondness and fair skin, long and thin faces, slender frames, and a strong sense of connectedness, no matter the physical distance between them.

David will come to see his younger sister as the best part of himself. She always brings out the best in him.

There are many childhood snapshots of the two of them together. In one, they are on tricycles on a sidewalk in front of a house, probably in Loudonville. Cynthia has her thumb or finger in her mouth; David is looking adoringly at his sister. As an adult, David will puckishly title this picture "Hell's Angels on Wheels."

In another photo, they are at the Workman / Stacher farm on East Main Street at the edge of Loudonville, standing near the corn crib—a cylindrical metal structure with a roof that resembles the hat of the "Tin Man" in the classic 1939 film "The Wizard of Oz." This structure is where ears of corn are stored. The crib wall is full of perforations that allow the air to pass freely while repelling the rain. In the corn crib photo, David is wearing his official Davy Crockett tee-shirt and Cynthia is dressed every bit the darling little girl in dressy shorts and anklet socks and patent leather shoes. Peeking out from behind Cynthia is David's cocker spaniel puppy named Candy—the first animal that David falls in love with, except the Teddy Bear species.

Their family makes a concerted effort to bring them together several times each year, because fate has dictated that they will never live closer than a 2½-hour drive apart.

David will grow up in Springfield. Cynthia will grow up in Loudonville and then, in high school, will move with Gene's family to Massillon when he becomes an officer in a bank in that steel-making city.

From 1951 until 1956, Cynthia will live with Rhea, their mother Hortense's friend and housekeeper, who moved back to Loudonville when George and little David disappeared in October of 1951.

While Gene is in the Navy, and visiting home on leave, he meets and falls in love with a gorgeous, outgoing brunette farm girl named Mickey Shearer from tiny McZena. In 1954, they marry while Gene is still serving in the Navy. They spend the first year of their marriage near Long Beach, California, where the Navy has stationed them.

When Gene's enlistment ends, Gene and Mickey move back home to Loudonville and begin their new life there. Gene finds work making bus luggage racks at the Flxible Company factory, until the head of Loudonville's bank calls Gene to convince him to become a teller at the bank. Olin Arnholt, like a lot of other folks in town, has had his eye on Gene. He likes what he has seen. Gene accepts the job offer at the bank, but to bring in more income, he also drives a school bus and operates the farm.

In about 1956, the police chief of Loudonville visits Gene at the bank and tells him that he received a report that George Laswell—Gene's stepfather and Cynthia's birth father—has absconded with a vehicle from a mission where he was living in a nearby state. The chief suggests that Gene keep a lookout in case George shows up in town.

This news prompts a local attorney to recommend to Gene and Mickey that they go through the legal steps to adopt Cynthia—just in case George should show up in town with ideas of leaving with Cynthia.

The court grants them adoption of Cynthia, and George never shows up in Loudonville or in Springfield.

Around Loudonville, and throughout the Workman family and Hortense's expansive family, Cynthia's adoption by Gene and Mickey is greeted with relief and jubilation.

The adoption is huge for Cynthia, and for Rhea. Sadly, Rhea will never again be on close terms with Hortense's family. However, Hortense's children will always love her, and will gather at her funeral in 1962, when she dies at age 63.

At the age of six, Cynthia begins a major life adjustment. Instead of being Gene's and Mickey's little sister, she is their daughter. They are, now and forever, Dad and Mom. And she has a baby brother, Mark—Gene's and Mickey's first-born.

One day, Cynthia packs a little bag and runs away from home at the farm on East Main Street. After a frantic search, she is found the same day a couple of miles away hiding next to the old abandoned one-room school where many of Hortense's Alsatian immigrant family members received their formal education.

Back home she goes, to live with Gene and Mickey.

Gradually, Cynthia makes the transition and fully becomes the oldest child of the Workmans' growing family. After Mark, then come Carol, Cathy and finally Cheryl. From day one, the children will regard Cynthia as their oldest sister. And she will embrace them, and love them, as her younger siblings. They will always be very, very close.

On a Sunday night in April 1958, Aunt Grace—the cousin who helped to rear Hortense during her growing-up years—writes a letter to Ralph Jr. and Louise in Springfield, from her home in Mount Vernon. In her beautiful, graceful penmanship, Grace relates the good reports that she has been receiving from Loudonville about the life that Gene and Mickey are giving Cynthia. Grace writes that Cynthia is well dressed, well cared for, and a "pretty little lady." Cynthia, along with all of Gene's and Mickey's family, regularly worships and attends Sunday School at Trinity Evangelical and Reformed Church. Grace adds, "How proud Hortense would be if she were living."

And Grace writes, "I am so glad that you folks have David. What would he have been if you folks hadn't found him, the poor little lad?"

David's own lasting memories of Loudonville begin in the summer of 1952, soon after Ralph Jr. and Louise bring him into their family.

They purchase a new suit for him, dress him up, and make the drive from Springfield to Loudonville to introduce their new son to people who will be important to him for the rest of his life.

They take him to a little farm north of Loudonville where Ralph Workman Sr. and his second wife, Marie, live and raise livestock and operate their kennel.

David's (and Ralph Jr.'s) brother, Jack, now lives at the farm with his father and stepmother. On this visit, or perhaps a later one, David will ride down the country roads with Jack in the teenager's Pontiac convertible, with the top down and the air blowing exhilaratingly into his face.

The pictures of this trip show Davy, dressed in a suit with a dual-tone dress coat, and a cap. He looks the perfect little gentleman, with no hint of the boy who, only recently, cussed like a sailor.

In the pictures, Ralph Jr. is dressed in his Sunday Best, with a jaunty neck tie. Louise is wearing a dark dress skirt, matching jacket, lacy bodice, and high heels.

Sixteen-year-old Jack sports a dress suit and Panama hat.

On the early visits to this little farm, David will sleep with Jack upstairs in the seemingly huge double bed, with its pile of soft bedding. One morning, David excitedly jumps up and down on the bed, flinging his little body into the air and provoking brother Jack to caution him: "Davy, you're making too much racket!"

David, and his new brother and sister, Danny and Peggy, will fondly remember the little farm, where they are warmly welcomed by Ralph Sr. and Marie. This is the place where Senior becomes "Big Dad" or "Granddad," and where Marie becomes "Grandma."

In these days, a photo is taken of a blended family gathered on the front porch of the little farm house. The picture is full of the possibilities that accompany new beginnings.

Peggy will have a favorite tree up on the hill behind the house. It is her special place. Danny will have a girlfriend down the road from the farm.

Marie welcomes three-year-old David and takes obvious, unaffected delight in him—fondly recalling the baths she gives him in the kitchen sink, and light-heartedly teasing him about his unique pronunciation of the word "turkey," which he renders as "tawwwkee."

And so it happens that David is accepted and welcomed as grandson by Hortense's ex-husband and by the woman he chose in her place.

For David, it will become a lifelong lesson about the power of grace and acceptance—the capacity of open arms and an open heart to transform human relationships.

The openness with which David is received by so many people will show him that every child absolutely matters.

One of David's earliest Christmas memories takes place at Ralph Sr.'s and Marie's little farm house. Junior and Louise, and David and Danny and Peggy, are in gathered in the living room in front of the Christmas tree.

They are opening wrapped gifts, and one in particular has David's attention. It is from Brother Gene, who is somewhere in the Pacific on the USS Helena. David tears it open, and beholds a beautifully crafted wooden speed boat, at least 18 inches long, adorned with intricate stainless steel fittings such as a propeller and horn and railings. To say the least, this little boy is very excited. Over the years, David—and eventually nephews—will love this wooden speedboat to death.

Most of David's lasting memories of Loudonville will include Cynthia.

Sometimes the two of them are playing in the old 1880s-era barn at the farm on East Main Street. In the barn, they may be climbing on, and burrowing through, the hay bales on the upper level, or feeding ears of corn through the antique hand-crank corn sheller and watching the kernels fly off the dry cobs. Or they may be upstairs in the barn, looking out across the pasture and firing "stick rifles" with imaginary bullets at imaginary attackers.

In one memory, they are playing upstairs in the barn, looking down through the trap door in the floor, where hay is dropped into the livestock area below. Suddenly, David jumps down into a pile of lose hay on the ground floor, and collapses as if dead or at least unconscious. Cynthia screams, and runs out the upper doorway, down the ramp and in through the lower door. "David," she yells, "are you okay?" As soon as she grabs him, he suddenly feigns consciousness with a big laugh. "You stinker!" she shouts.

Of such things, memories to last a lifetime are made in the barn built by Granddad Ralph Workman Sr.'s grandparents, David and Rebecca Stacher.

Another time, Gene is out in a pasture, inspecting the newly dug fence post holes, when he spots a tiny whitetail deer fawn in a post hole. It has been hidden here by its mother. Gene reaches down and lifts it from the hole, bringing the fawn into his arms. In doing so, he has adopted the fawn, which will become imprinted on these humans.

Soon, the fawn has a human name: Princess. Cynthia, the visiting David, and the other kids will know the thrill of feeding Princess from a rubber-nippled milk bottle—and the ticklish feeling of Princess sucking on their ears. Laughter abounds at these times.

Before many months have passed, Gene realizes that he has created a cute little spotted, white-tailed eating machine, which mows down the flowers and shrubs growing on the human-owned properties along East Main Street on the outskirts of Loudonville.

Finally, the day comes when Gene loads a doe named Princess into one of the farm vehicles and drives her out to the state forest, where he releases her—and says his final goodbye. He can only hope that Princess will find out how to survive the natural predators and two-legged hunters with rifles.

Loudonville summers are filled with memories, including rock skipping and picnics at Mohican State Park, Gene's swim lessons at Long Lake beach, and bouncy walks across the swinging suspension bridge over the Clear Fork of the Mohican River.

Loudonville winters create more memories—sledding down the snowy hill at Mickey's parents' farm at McZena, and skating on the frozen pond down the road from the East Main Street farm with Cynthia and cousins Gloria, Peggy and Cindy.

One Christmas season, David has the good luck to be in Loudonville at just the right time to participate in the "Great Christmas Tree Hunt in the Forest."

Gene and the kids climb into the station wagon and drive forest roads, looking for just the right specimen of an evergreen tree to grace the living room of the farm, with its sky-high ceilings.

That night, David stands in the cavernous living room, gazing up at 10 or 11 feet of Christmas tree and lights and decorations.

It is a magical moment that shapes Christmases for decades to come. As a husband and a father, David will go out with his own family each year to Christmas tree farms. Bucksaw in hand, they will search for the perfect fir to fill their home with the smells and lights of the season.

In a very real sense, David will be a Loudonville boy his entire life, although Springfield is the city that will give him the opportunities that will propel him through life.

First trip to visit new grandparents with
new parents

David becomes reacquainted with brother Jack

David at the farm with his two best friends

At joyous times when they're together,
David's eyes are on Cynthia

Dan, Jack, Gene, Grandmother Marie,
Grandfather Ralph Sr., Peggy

—13—
The All-American Childhood of One American Boy

David's life may have started out differently from most of the kids he knows, but as soon as he arrives in Louise's and Ralph's life, that all changes.

In addition to his family in Loudonville, he gains a sister and brother in Springfield, plus aunts, uncles, cousins and grandparents who are Louise's extended family in Nashville, Tennessee, and Paducah, Kentucky.

In time, sister Peggy marries brother-in-law Dan Quinn, and there are *two* Dans in his family. Peggy and Dan make David an uncle three times over, as Tim, then Steve, then Cathy are born.

Brother Dan marries Judy, and they make David an uncle three more times—to Greg, Darrell and Bradley.

Many a childhood weekend will be spent with brothers, sisters, nephews and nieces.

As David loves his trips to be with Cynthia and family in Loudonville, she is thrilled by her visits to Springfield to be with David and family. Both of them love their times together, and hate saying goodbye. However, they love the sense of belonging in two families.

At the end of one visit to Springfield in 1968, 18-year-old Cynthia writes a note to her brother Ralph Jr., sister-in-law Louise, and brother David.

"It was so wonderful coming down & as usual I hate to leave," she writes, "but yet my folks are waiting for me. I feel so lucky having 2 of the <u>greatest</u> families in the world as mine—seriously!"

Forty-six years after Cynthia writes this note, David will find it again in a 1965 Converse sneakers box, its lid tied on with a string. The box is full of notes and letters from young Cynthia to David in Springfield.

Re-reading the note about "2 of the greatest families in the world," David, now a father and grandfather, is struck by how Cynthia had always been so keenly aware of family and of relationships, of all that matters most.

She summed up, in a few words, what was so great about being David and Cynthia Workman. After losing their mother and being abandoned by their birth father, each of them gained not one family that loved and cared for them, but two.

Gene's and Mickey's children Mark, Carol, Cathy and Cheryl are David's nephew and nieces. But because they are Cynthia's siblings, they become, in a way, David's siblings.

David's brother and sister, Danny and Peggy, become Cynthia's siblings as well.

One day, after Gene and Mickey and family have moved to Massillon, Ohio, Gene introduces David to a business associate. "I would like you to meet my brother, Dave," Gene says. The associate replies: "Oh, so you're Cynthia's uncle?" While David's mind is spinning for how to answer, Gene replies simply: "Something like that."

It proves to be perfectly elegant way of sparing a casual acquaintance an unneeded information overload, on a street corner in Massillon, Ohio.

As a child, David doesn't think about how lucky he is. He is blessedly free to make the most of being a kid in 1950s and 1960s America.

Ralph Jr. and Louise, now known to him exclusively as Dad and Mom, will demonstrate an uncanny ability to surprise David by demonstrating an interest in all of his activities.

Early in David's second grade year, the little boy can't believe his eyes one morning at McKinley Elementary School. There, coming down the hallway, is a familiar big, tall man. "Why are you here, Dad?" he asks excitedly. To which Ralph answers: "To have lunch with you."

And sure enough, Ralph joins David's second-grade class in the lunchroom. He scoots his six-foot-four-inch frame onto the little lunch table and benches, right there among the little kids. And when all the lunches have been eaten, Ralph buys every kid at the table an ice cream bar. It will be a rich and recurring memory.

And later, when David joins Cub Scouts and eventually graduates to Boy Scouts, there will never be a single time when David's parents miss one of his awards ceremonies. When he gets his Bobcat pin at age 10, they are there. When he gets his Wolf Badge, his Bear Badge, his Lion Badge, his Webelos (later to be called Arrow of Light) Badge, they are there. In Boy Scouts, when he gets his Tenderfoot Badge, his Second Class Badge, his First Class Badge, his Star Badge, his Life Badge, they are there.

When David is stalled in his Scout advancement to First Class because he hasn't passed the 50-yard swim requirement, Ralph takes the initiative and arranges to have son-in-law Dan Quinn serve as the swim coach / evaluator for this activity. Off they go to the Springfield Springs swim club, where Dan patiently coaches David to a successful completion of the necessary laps. Finally, David is a First Class Scout, and qualified for the more advanced (and fun) outdoor adventures in Boy Scouts.

As a high school student, teenage David will often not think of mentioning some special event at school. And thus, on the day when David is called up on the stage in the Springfield South High School auditorium to be admitted into the National Honor Society, he will be shocked to see—out in the auditorium audience—his dad, his mom and sister Peggy.

After the ceremony, he asks why they are here, but somewhere inside, he is proud that they are.

At the Workman house in Springfield, Thanksgiving and Christmas holidays are filled with family, food, and traditions. But nothing will top Christmas.

On the night before Christmas in 1955, a very excited six-year-old David takes a bath in the claw foot tub, complete with his little floating toys. Tonight, he doesn't linger in the water. He is a boy with a mission. He dresses and is tucked into bed with good-night kisses, but he can hardly contain himself. His head is racing with the words and tune of "Santa Claus Is Coming to Town." He cannot go to sleep.

And then, Big Brother Danny shows up in his room. "David, get up," he says urgently. "There's somebody next door who wants to see you."

Jumping out of bed, the six-year-old throws his clothes on. Next door they go to the Groebers' big house on Belmont Avenue.

Paul and Catherine Groeber are wonderful people with a big German Catholic family—12 children plus grandchildren, with more grandkids coming each year. Every day, but especially at Christmas time, the Groeber house is a village unto itself. And David is among those who are welcome into this village.

On this Christmas Eve, when Danny takes David next door to their house, a huge surprise awaits. There, by the bricked fireplace in the living room, sits Santa Claus. The actual Santa Claus! Not a department store Santa. This is the real thing!

One by one, Santa welcomes each of the youngest children of the village onto his lap. David gets his turn. These moments with the real Santa will brighten all of David's future Christmases with a heart-pumping memory.

Beginning in 1957, David's Christmas Eves will take place on Beacon Street in Springfield—where he spends most of his childhood. Each year, he and his dad relish going out and picking out the Christmas tree from one of the lots in town, then carefully erecting the tree in its stand. They wrap the colored electric lights around the tree—being careful not to burn themselves on the colored lights, which get so hot that the paint sometimes peels off the surface of the bulbs. And then David has the job of hanging the delicate ball ornaments, the Santas, the glass pine cones, the foil icicles, and special decorations—some of which he himself has made with his own hands.

On the radio, Christmas songs are playing—traditional carols as well as timeless hits by Bing Crosby, Doris Day, Patti

Page, Perry Como, and many more. Meanwhile, Louise—Mom—is decorating the living room and the dining room with treasured decorations. These include the Yule Log candle holder that David made by drilling holes with a hand-crank brace and bit, then painting it green and gluing glitter in all the right places.

Each year of David's childhood, he will spend most every night of the Christmas season lying on the dining room floor, in the glow of the Christmas tree, taking it all in and singing along with the songs on the radio.

In the 1950s and 1960s, Springfield is a good place for a boy to grow up. It's big enough to have distinct neighborhoods, each with its own personality, and lots of manufacturing jobs that pay good family wages.

From the Workman house on Beacon Street, downtown is walking distance or easy biking distance (a couple of miles). And farmland is even closer.

Summers are the best.

After the mowing, weeding, yard cleanup and similar chores are completed to Mom's exacting specifications, David is free to play with the neighborhood guys each summer day. The main rules are: come home for lunch and dinner, and be back home before dark. And do not be out of earshot when Mom comes out and calls the words "David Leeeeeeee."

In the neighborhood, everything a kid might want to do is within easy walking distance, although the kids spend half their lives on their bikes. Make that three-fourths.

One block up the street is the elementary school where David will spend four and a half of his school years, from second grade through sixth grade. There, he will get to be on the school traffic patrol for a year. He will become long-term friends with teacher Doug Hemry, who notes David's love of nature and who kindles a lifelong interest in forestry.

In a future time, David will work for the Washington State Department of Natural Resources, the forestry agency. Not as a forester, but as a communicator and educator.

In elementary school, Mr. Hemry also recruits David to write for the school "newspaper," a mimeographed sheet called "Kenwood Speaks."

One more block past Kenwood Heights Elementary, the Springfield School District builds a new junior high for seventh, eighth and ninth grades. They name it for Benjamin Franklin. This being the heart of the Cold War, the brand-new school is built with a bomb shelter in the ground beneath the classrooms. Air Raid Drills are frequent. When they occur, the kids are all filed down into the ground to practice bomb survival.

On the grounds of these two schools, there is ample playground equipment and room for baseball and football pickup games organized by the neighborhood kids. And, boy, are there plenty of kids in the neighborhood.

Many, like David, live in two-story houses (three, if you include the basement that every house is built over). Many of these were built in the years between the World Wars. Many kids live in newer single-story houses built in the '40s and '50s and '60s.

Here and there, in this part of Springfield in the 1950s and 1960s, there are patches of woodland, each with its special allure. They're alive with the likes of maple, mulberry, oak and buckeye. One woodland is reachable just out the back door and through his buddy Denny's yard. Another is a couple of blocks farther across Selma Road, and in the middle of it is "the castle"—a house much larger and more estate-like than any other in this part of Springfield.

Several blocks the other direction, down Kenton Street, there's a special patch of woods occupying a hill known to the kids as the Indian Mound. It's true that the Mound Builder cultures did occupy Ohio centuries before, but whether they had any hand in creating the wooded mound at Kenton Street is not known to David and his friends. They just believe it is so, and that is enough to make it special. Besides, there is a good vantage point for watching through the trees at the cars as they drive by on Kenton Street and on Burnett Road. Later, the woods will be cut down and a care facility will be built onto and into the mound.

In good weather the kids ride up and down the streets—especially DOWN the streets that are built on hills. A favorite technique is Riding with No Hands. It is imperative to master this technique so you can make all your necessary hand and arm gestures.

A bicycle also makes it possible to ride to more far-away destinations in the neighborhood. Such as The Pond. The boys cannot resist the lure of the neighborhood's favorite wetland. They do not call it a wetland, however; it is simply The Pond.

One summer, the boys get the idea of building a raft and asking Denny's dad to haul it for them to The Pond. His dad, a carpenter by trade, provides the wood, the tools, and the nails; and he lets the boys figure out together how a raft is made.

First they nail together a frame. Then they nail boards across the frame. Then someone points out that it isn't very high, and they might get wet. So the boys build another layer or two on top of the frame—and then they nail down more planks across the top. Finally, the boys declare their satisfaction, and deem the raft complete. It stands at least two feet tall, maybe two and a half. It's probably four feet by four feet. Basically, it resembles a square layer cake.

When he gets home from work, Denny's dad dutifully examines the raft, and agrees to haul it to The Pond in the next day or so. There is something about the look on his countenance that David will think about in the years ahead.

The day comes when it's time to float The Raft on The Pond. Denny's dad hauls it a mile or so to the water. The boys eagerly make their way to water's edge, and begin dragging their custom-built watercraft out into the depths. It sinks straight to the bottom.

Hmmmm. How did that happen? The boys discuss the question among themselves. Denny's dad has that look on his face again. It's a look that seems to say: "Do you boys think it might be too tall and heavy for the amount of water surface?"[xvii]

The boys have learned a first-hand lesson about buoyancy. However, their raft building days are done. There are many other things to do with the days of summer in Springfield, Ohio.

Even nights are fun in summer. At night, you can sit outside with the family, watching fireflies light up the night, and you can catch them. Only nobody calls them fireflies. They're lightning bugs, of course.

Also within walking distance of the Workman home are at least three mom-and-pop grocery stores where a growing boy can fuel his cells with soda pop, ice cream bars, Popsicles, O'Henry bars, and root beer barrel candies.

In the '60s, a new shopping area is built a few blocks away on Selma Road. It's called Southern Village Shopping Center, reflecting the fact that it is in one of the South End neighborhoods of Springfield. Southern Village has a pharmacy, a couple of department or five-and-dime stores, a hardware store, a Big Bear supermarket, a barber shop, a book store / liquor store, and a branch of the Warder Public Library.

Though David is blissfully unaware of it, this is a sign of the future. The downtown shopping area of Springfield, like almost every other downtown in America, is doomed as a retail center. Shopping centers are coming, and they will be getting bigger and bigger.

David and his adolescent buddies will frequent all of the stores at Southern Village (except the liquor department of the book store), but the one that will have the biggest impact on David is the library branch. Every week or so, he will browse the history and the geography sections of the library branch, picking out his next free book, which will take him on a journey through time and place. Without realizing it, David becomes a lover of the written word.

The Springfield home where David does
most of his growing up

Mickey Workman, daughter Cheryl and son Mark at the
historic Workman Cabin in Loudonville, 2013

—14—
First Jobs

For a couple of years, David will earn spending money by carrying the written word to 40 or 50 houses around the neighborhood. He will be a newspaper carrier for Springfield's morning paper, The Sun.

A week's subscription costs 42 cents, and David will visit his customers' houses each week, learning two important life skills—computing math in his head and making change, plus knowing when certain elusive customers are most likely to be home and unable to evade their young bill collector.

The newspaper carrier's profit on each paper is a few cents. In the '60s, it will do just fine.

Sometimes, in these early 1960s, a customer's payment will include a coin that goes straight into his amateur coin collection, such as an Indian Head Penny, which were minted from 1859 through 1909, or a Steel Penny (steel coated with zinc), which were minted in 1943 when copper was needed for military shell casings to support the war effort. David keeps his coin collection in his official Roy Rogers Lunch Box, which no self-respecting seventh grader would take to school.

As a paper boy, David gets up before daylight six days per week, retrieving the bundle of papers off the porch and stuffing them carefully, one by one, into his canvas delivery bag. David learns about deadlines. The morning paper must be on the customer's front porch before the customer is likely to sit down at the breakfast table.

He learns important details of customer service. For example, the newspaper must not be on the front sidewalk or the front step or the driveway. It must be on the front porch. Anything less is lousy customer service, and the delivery boy will receive a phone call from his counselor (boss) at the News and Sun. For some customers, the ones who tip David a nickel or so during his weekly collection circuit, the paper will be nicely tucked into the door, or in the wire frame that hangs beneath the mail slot of some mailboxes that are mounted under the porch roof of many customers' houses.

There are some fringe benefits of delivering newspapers by bicycle and by foot in the 1960s. David becomes adept at rolling up a newspaper and tucking it inside itself so it won't blow apart on the porches of Springfield. After a while, he doesn't even have to look at the motion of his hands; it becomes one smooth, automatic process while walking up to the house. And then comes the day when David gets that miracle of American technology—his first hand-sized, battery-powered transistor radio. Now, when he walks or rides the neighborhood on those early mornings, David can tune into the Top 40 channel and hear the songs that make America great. Songs like the Everly Brothers' "Bowling Green."

Although he doesn't know it at the time, those early mornings wrestling newspapers have another lasting effect. It so happens that David must arise for newspaper counting just about the time that his dad is getting ready to drive to Schwermann Trucking Company, where Ralph Jr. will work most of his driving career.

This means Dad is the one to get him out of bed, and father and son often have a few minutes together before Dad heads off to pick up his cement-hauling semi-tractor trailer. These minutes together forge a bond that will never be broken—not even in the "crazy teen years" ahead.

One more establishment in the Kenwood Heights / Selma Road area of Springfield will play a big role in David's life.

River Dale Dairy, in mid-century Springfield, is a beloved institution. In its two-story block building on Selma Road at Oak Street are concocted the milk and ice cream and cottage cheese products that delight thousands of customers.

On a summer night, dozens of people line up waiting their turn for a double-dip cone or a milk shake or sundae at River Dale's chest-high, stainless-steel ice cream counter. The line often snakes through the dairy store, out the front door, around the parking lot, out to the curb of Selma Road.

Customers gladly wait and pay 12 cents, later 15 cents, for River Dale's ice cream double-dip taste delights.

One day in about February of his sophomore year at Springfield South High School, David Workman walks into River Dale Dairy, and is issued his apron and oh-so-manly white food handlers' cap. He is the newest part-time employee, earning the princely sum of 85 cents an hour. After a probationary period, he gets a 40-cent pay raise. For the first time, David will have enough money to buy his own clothes—or at least to put them on layaway to be taken home when he finishes paying for them. In a time before credit cards, layaway makes it possible to purchase bigger-ticket items on a payment schedule.

During his three years or so dipping ice cream cones, stacking heavy cases of glass milk bottles, packaging ice cream, tending the cottage cheese vat, and cleaning stainless steel dairy production equipment, David learns many life lessons.

Take, for example, the busy summer night when a customer complains to the owner, Mr. Paul Gram, about something David has or hasn't done to his satisfaction. Mr. Gram summons David to his office, explains his displeasure, and fires the young fellow on the spot. A stunned teenager heads to the small, cramped male-employee locker room to change into his "street clothes." His mind is racing, but he is, for the moment, rather numb.

David is pulling off his white dairy uniform when the door opens. There sits Mr. Gram in his wheelchair.

"Dave," the dairy owner says, apologetically, "Bonnie (she is one of River Dale Dairy's trusted full-time employees) told me what really happened out there. I would appreciate it if you would stay. I don't want you to leave."

David takes no time in responding: "Thank you, Mr. Gram. I would like to stay."

When the door closes again and Mr. Gram wheels himself out to the front sales room, the newly rehired ex-employee breathes a sigh of relief. He silently files away a mental note that his respect for the owner of River Dale Dairy has just gotten even higher.

At that, David dons his white uniform and apron again, and returns to work behind the ice cream counter, scooping up double-dip 15-cent cones that are a taster's delight. The other kids working the dairy this night look surprised to see him back. They, too, are relieved.

Tonight, dairy work has taught David some things the young man will remember long into his life.

It's okay—in fact, more than okay—to admit you have made a mistake, even when you're the boss. In fact, especially when you're the boss.

And, as off-duty co-worker Bonnie has shown, sometimes you have to stand up for other people when you see an injustice being done.

For the next 48 years, David will be in America's work force almost continually. Although it doesn't mean anything to him at the time, David is now officially enrolled in, and paying into, the marvelous American invention known as Social Security. A lifetime into the future, David will silently thank Mr. Gram for taking a chance on him, and for investing him in America's best investment program.

It is one of the important "firsts" in an American life.

—15—
Guiding Lights

In any happy life, at least among humans, there are guiding lights—people who show you the way to go, and the way to be. David will come to realize how many he has, and how much he owes to them.

Louise

His mom, Louise, will be among the very first lights in his life. Whereas his mother Hortense gave him life and cared for him in his first 13 months in the world, Louise will give him a safe place to become himself. She will be his compass, always pointing to True North. She will also be his Knower of Truths—selecting exactly the right words to say to him at exactly the right time.

She demonstrates this amazing capacity in March of 1981, all of 29 years after taking David in as her son and one of her three children. One morning, he is at her bedside in Springfield's Community Hospital, where she is awaiting a heroic attempt at surgery to save her from cancer.

She is very sick, and she must be very weak and apprehensive. But it is her strength and clarity that shine through in these moments before she is wheeled away. Somehow, Louise has managed a few precious moments with David, alone together in her hospital room.

At this moment, David is feeling confused and vulnerable and almost lost. His mom is so sick, and for the first and last time in his career, David is unemployed. His employer, the Everett Herald, has been sold; and some of the people who were acquired in the purchase agreement are no longer deemed necessary to the operation of the newspaper.

David also is a young husband and a father of two little girls, worrying about how he will make a living to support them.

And so it is that Louise looks at him through the eyes of love from her hospital bed. She proceeds to tell him, in detail, how proud she is of him. She reveals that, when Ralph Jr. made that drive to Alabama to retrieve the lost little boy in 1952, there were people who didn't think she should take on responsibility for a child who was not her own.

The naysayers were wrong, she says to David. She tells him that he has turned out to be a fine person, a good man, a good father and husband. She would not change a thing. There is absolutely no doubt at this moment that David matters, that David is loved, and that his life is a success.

The mom who gave him everything that a child needs is now giving a man what only she can give—a mother's clarity. In this moment in the hospital, and in every moment of the remaining decades of David's life, Louise's light shines brightly. Thirty-four years later, she still shows him who he is.

Ralph Jr. and Gene

The two most formative men in David's life will always be the first two who stood tall for him, back when he was a helpless infant and toddler.

As a grown man looking back, David will come to understand that his second-oldest brother, Gene, must have made a profound impression on him. Gene was, after all, the boy-man who held Hortense's family together for as long as he could after her death-too-young. As a very small boy, when he saw the framed photos of Machinist's Mate Gene Workman in his Navy uniform, David knew exactly who the man in the picture was. The man was his hero.

Later, after Ralph and Louise had taken David into their family and after Gene and Mickey had taken Cynthia into their family, David would have frequent opportunities to observe and absorb Gene Workman's gracious, easygoing way of relating to other people.

He would recognize Gene as a hard worker, a respected member of the community, a playful and totally involved father, and an extraordinary leader. As an adult visiting brother Gene at the banks where he would serve as an officer, David would observe his respectful way of dealing with others—employees, customers, business acquaintances, anyone at all.

In a 1997 interview with the Wooster Daily Record, bank executive Gene Workman would be quoted as explaining his core philosophy as a manager and leader: "I learned a long time ago you cannot lead people in a direction they do not want to go."[xviii]

In a talk that same year with students at his alma mater, Loudonville High School, Gene would tell the students that, while he had much help from others throughout his life, he had learned that "the best place to look for a helping hand is at the end of your own arms."

From his brother Gene and from his brother-turned-dad Ralph, David will learn about forgiveness and redemption. He sees how they find it within themselves to forgive their father, Ralph Sr., twice—for divorcing their mother and leaving the family, and for getting a court order that took the Loudonville farm from his three sons, who had inherited it from their Grandmother Workman.

During David's high school years, one of the hit songs in the Top 40 is sung by many artists, most notably The Hollies. Named for the motto of Boys Town in Nebraska, the title is "He Ain't Heavy, He's My Brother." This song will always touch David to his very core, with its instrumentation and especially its lyrics, which declare that an unnamed brother is "my concern," and that he isn't a burden to bear.

He receives it as an anthem to the brothers and sisters who were willing to bear any burden in order to save David and Cynthia, and to give them each a great life.

The very best version of "He Ain't Heavy" will be sung many years later, especially for David, by his brother, Dan Workman Welch, a gifted singer.

From the brothers Ralph and Gene, young David also learns not to be a slacker and not to be a pushy, aggressive leader. Pushiness might work for some people, but not for the Workman boys.

David would learn that persuasion is better than bossiness, and that self-persuasion is even better. In other words, the best results come when people decide for themselves to choose the right path.

Ralph would splendidly illustrate the power of self-persuasion when David, a teenager, gets tired of driving around in the ugliest car in town—a greenish-gray 1950 Nash Statesman flathead six-cylinder. The best description for a 1950 Nash would be "tank" (as in Army tank) or "inverted bathtub."

In its place, David has the idea of spending his dairy paychecks on buying a little Honda motorcycle. He tells his dad, and makes the case for how it will pencil out within his available income.

Ralph unequivocally likes the Nash because it's solid and it has a cracked engine head that prevents the car from exceeding 50 miles per hour—downhill. Also, he just likes Nashes and, in fact, has one himself. However, Ralph does not attempt to talk his headstrong teenager out of buying the motorcycle of his dreams.

Instead, Ralph says: "That's an idea worth thinking about, son. Give it two weeks' thought, and then let's talk about it."

David is surprised, but pleased, that he hasn't gotten an outright "no way in heck are you going to buy a death machine on two wheels!" So he agrees to come back in two weeks.

Two weeks later, the dream of speeding around Springfield is no longer rattling around in his cranium. The subject never comes up again.

Score one for Dad.

Another brilliant example of self-persuasion as a leadership strategy occurs during the one and only time when David's dad is serving on the bargaining committee for his Teamsters' Union local. After this experience in an elected position, Ralph Workman Jr. declares he has had enough of politics and will never hold an office again. He doesn't.

It is fortunate, however, that Ralph is serving on the bargaining committee when the union leadership reaches a tentative agreement with the trucking company, for pay raises, vacation and other benefits.

Ralph and the union leaders know they have gotten a great agreement, but a small group in the local membership decide to fight it. Ralph's view is that they're angling to defeat the contract and get elected as bargaining unit officers in the next election.

The vocal faction is starting to get traction with the membership ahead of the ratification vote. So, as Ralph retells the story years later, he suggests sending to every member's home address a brief summary of the pay raise, vacation days, and other benefits in the tentative agreement. The summary is factual, not argumentative. But instead of mailing it in an envelope, the union mails it as a post card. This means spouses or anyone else who has access to the post card will see with their own eyes what a good deal it is. The contract is overwhelmingly ratified.

Ralph chuckles when he recalls how drivers who opposed the contract complained to him about those darn post cards. They didn't appreciate having to answer to their wives, lobbying them to vote for the contract. One of the drivers said to him: "Workman, even the mail man told me I'd better vote for that contract."

Why tell people what they should do when they can arrive at that conclusion on their own, perhaps with a little help?

Neither Gene nor Ralph, however, has any problem acting decisively if and when that's needed.

Ralph demonstrates this when teenage David embarrasses the family with some of his impertinent behavior. On this occasion, David argues with his father and discovers that he has pushed the limits too far. For the only time in his life, his Dad pokes his long, strong index finger into David's sternum, creating a percussion-like effect and leaving the son exactly one recourse: back down right now and knock off the impertinence. It is unforgettable because Ralph has never been so riled at him before. And because he has a right to be.

On another occasion in high school, David gets his dander up about some issue or another and writes a "letter to the editor" of the local newspaper. His intention is to see his letter published on the editorial, or opinion, page of the paper.

Ralph has made it his business to read the letter, and he doesn't see how any good can come to his son from having this particular opinion published for thousands of people to read. So he volunteers to take care of mailing it. The son thanks him.

A few weeks later, after watching every day to see his opinions expressed in the newspaper, he mentions his disappointment to his dad. And Ralph says, "I didn't mail it."

"What?" David says. "Why not?"

"Because I didn't think it was an appropriate letter to have published in the newspaper," his dad responds.

The teenager is briefly disappointed, but eventually, he admits to himself: "Dad was right."

In this case, the father has served as the top editor for his son. Later in life, David will have many editors and although he won't always agree with every decision, he will never doubt their importance in saving his bacon.

In a future era of instant, ubiquitous communication through social media and cyberspace—a time when anybody can say or write anything to thousands or millions of people, with no reviews and no editors—David will think to himself that editors are a very good thing, indeed.

Alice Wolf

In September 1966, on the first school day in David's senior year, David gets an unwelcome surprise. All summer, he has looked forward to being in the Yearbook Class at Springfield South High School. These are the kids who produce "The Wildcat," the spectacular book full of pictures and captions that 600-plus members of the Class of 1967 will cherish forever.

Not only does he look forward to taking pictures and writing copy for the high-production-value "Wildcat," but he looks forward to being in class and working with the other kids who will produce this yearbook. He knows many of them, and he likes them a lot.

On this first morning of senior year, looking at his class schedule, David cannot believe that the people in charge at South High have made a schedule change without his permission. He is very grumpy that he won't be a part of Yearbook Class even though he is assigned to Yearbook Home Room. The injustice of it all!

To top it off, the school officials have unilaterally assigned him to Journalism Class, the group of kids who produce the South High Herald, which every student and faculty member receives automatically, and which very few of them will keep more than a few days.

David makes up his mind. When he shows up in Journalism Class today, he will exercise his right to withdraw from the class and request a schedule change to some other class. He is adamant about this.

He has not taken into account one factor—Mrs. Alice Wolf, the teacher who over the summer was appointed to be the Journalism teacher and South High Herald advisor for the 1966-67 school year.

That afternoon, when he marches into the journalism class on the south side of the massive, monumental, domed sandstone structure known as South High School, he plops down in a metal-framed desk that is located just about dead-center in the classroom.

He looks around, surveying the class as kids arrive. He recognizes many of them, but he doesn't know most of them personally. There's Floyd Wolfenbarger, a friend from Debate Team and other classes. There's Eddie Howard, who has a razor-sharp wit. There's Bob Headley, a really cool and friendly guy.

In a few minutes, Mrs. Wolf steps up in front, welcomes the students, and promptly lays out her dynamic vision for the class, for the Herald newspaper, and the for the exciting year that she and the students will create.

When she has finished her brief but invigorating pep talk, David silently tells himself: "I'll give this two weeks, and then I can pull out." Two weeks is the deadline for making a schedule change at South High.

A couple of days later, Mrs. Wolf makes her staffing assignments for producing the South High Herald. Everybody will have an important job assignment in order to make the Herald the best newspaper it can be. The class's customers, the students and faculty of South High, deserve everybody's very best.

In truth, the Herald is a high-end publication with book-quality paper and professional pressmanship, produced every other week on a hot-lead printing press downstairs in this very building.

David is assigned to be one of two Co-Editors, the other being his buddy, Floyd. He will be writing articles of his own, editing the articles of other staff members, and writing editorials. Yes, the Herald has an editorial page.

The two weeks come and go, and David never gives another thought to a schedule change. Mrs. Wolf has him hooked. Every day is exciting, challenging, fast-moving and fun. Oh yes, and every class is packed full of learning.

Although high school students don't get paid for going to class, Alice Wolf's journalism class is not an amateur operation. While you are producing a weekly newspaper, you are learning the fundamentals of journalism as it is practiced in real newspapers, radio stations and television networks across America.

From her, the students learn how to write a compelling "lead (pronounced lede) paragraph" containing the "four w's" of journalism—"who, what, when and where."

You learn how to write a compelling, accurate headline—not always easy when there is so little space for large type fonts.

You learn to write photo captions (or "cutlines" as they're called in the news business).

Sometime during the year, Mrs. Wolf arranges for the class to meet with Norman Pearson, who is the city editor of the Springfield Daily News. He gives an inspiring, entertaining talk. He tells a funny story about a headline writing contest in which the writers had been challenged to write the highest-impact headline possible within the limitations of the font size and the narrow column width.

The winning headline, according to Mr. Pearson: "Pope Elopes."

He gets a big laugh from the high school journalism class. This first encounter with a professional newspaperman makes a lasting, positive impression on Co-Editor David Workman.

Journalism class at South High School turns out to be so much fun that David has no qualms at all about staying after school in the journalism classroom, doing his part to make the Herald the best newspaper it can be. On press day, he joins Mrs. Wolf in the press room downstairs, to spot-check the "press run" and give the official green light to complete that week's printing of a few thousand newspapers.

In the spring of 1967, James Rhodes is inaugurated Governor of Ohio. He is an alumnus of this very school, and attended classes in this very building. The South High choir is invited to perform at one of the inaugural events in Columbus, and David is assigned to go along as the newspaper correspondent covering the event for the Herald.

David is given his first "press pass" credential, and takes copious notes during Governor Rhodes' inaugural speech. Along with the other students, he receives a commemorative plate that will occupy a cupboard in the Workman household for decades to come. And back at South High, David writes a news article for the Herald—his first news story about politics and government in America.

Meanwhile, Eddie Howard has gotten himself hired at the Springfield newspaper, as an actual professional journalist, going to work after school. He has his own assigned desk, telephone, and everything, on the third floor of the imposing News and Sun Building downtown.

One day that spring, at the close of the school day, David is chatting with Mrs. Wolf before going to work at River Dale Dairy.

This is when the teacher asks, "What will you do after you graduate?"

"I'm going to college," he replies.

"What do you want to become after college?" she asks.

"Oh, I don't know. Maybe a teacher."

"Do you like writing?" she asks. "Do you like writing for a newspaper?"

"Yes, I do," David says.

"Have you ever considered newspaper writing for a living?

"No, I guess I haven't."

"Well," she asks, "what do you think about it?"

Pausing a moment, he says: "I guess I would like that."

From this moment forward, David knows he wants to be a writer, a reporter, an editor. In a later era, he will expand that definition to include "communicator."

Although David doesn't know it yet, Alice Wolf and her husband Tom will become practically members of his family, and vice versa. Daughters Kara and Kirsten will know them intimately as "Aunt Alice" and "Uncle Tom."

David and Alice will talk often, on the phone, right up to a few days before her death at age 92 in 2013.

In June 1967, the South High School Class of 1967 graduation / commencement ceremony takes place at Springfield's majestic Memorial Hall.

The Workman family is there, of course, proud and elated that the little boy they made their own is now on his way to being a man in his own right.

From Mrs. Wolf's first high school journalism class, Eddie Howard will go on to a career with the Associated Press, where he will become a political reporter to be reckoned with in Lincoln, the capital of Nebraska. Bob Headley will earn a doctoral degree and become a professor of English and philosophy, teaching courses in literature, film, creative writing, composition, and technical writing. Floyd Wolfenbarger will become an inspirational pastor and preacher in the Freewill Baptist Church.

After the 1967 graduation ceremony, outside the Hall, Mrs. Wolf poses for a picture with David in his cap and gown. Ralph is the photographer.

Ralph thanks Mrs. Wolf for all she has done for David. Mrs. Wolf congratulates David's parents. Many years later, she will recall for David a question that his dad asked her that day: "Do you think David can make a living as a writer?" Without hesitation, she told him: "Yes, I do."

Early newspaper editors and mentors

On the night in November 1968 when David Workman first reports for duty at the Springfield Sun, he is full of excitement and eager anticipation, but he has no way of knowing how his life and career and values will be shaped by the generation of men and women who direct news gathering and news reporting for Springfield's morning newspaper.

Looking back, he will one day realize that these people were examples of what NBC broadcaster / author Tom Brokaw would call the Greatest Generation of Americans.

Four in particular will influence him, in part because of the long hours they will spend together five nights per week, beginning between 2 o'clock and 4 o'clock. Allan Barth, Joe Gray, Larry Brown (Brownie), and Maynard (Mike) Kniskern are men of great intelligence and principle, serious about the responsibility they have to provide accurate, factual, fair and interesting information to the readers of The Sun every day. They also have good hearts. They care about people, including cub reporters like David Workman.

This generation of newspaper editors has been shaped by their experience as military inductees in World War II. Sometimes, late at night after the daily newspaper has been "put to bed"—while everyone is waiting for the first proofing run to come off the presses—these military veterans will share stories and anecdotes about things they experienced and life lessons they learned in the service of their country. There's no bragging, only reflecting.

Several months into David's journalism career, Joe calls the young man into an office, chats with him about his future, and tells him, "You have executive potential." From this day forward, David is empowered to see himself in a different way.

One night while the editors are waiting for the paper to come off the presses, the conversation turns to the regrettable things that some people say, in writing, in the newspaper. Joe explains how he avoids printing something that he will regret.

"Whenever I write something while I'm hot under the collar," the editor says, "I put it in a drawer overnight. The next morning, I look at it in the cold light of day. Then I decide whether I still want to say it."

Often, the editor reflects, "I put it into the round file."

The young writer mentally files another lesson away. Many times in the years to come, he will "round-file" something that sounded really good when he wrote it in the passion of the moment.

Allan—or Al, as he is called in the newsroom—will leave a special legacy to David and other young reporters, in the form of short notes that he will type out, each on a "half sheet" of copy paper with his initials—"agb". Each note will comment on something that Al has liked about the young journalist's work that day. David will appreciate the notes, and will keep them in his boxes of ancient, musty newspaper memorabilia. More importantly, perhaps, Allan Barth has quietly influenced how the young professional will encourage and motivate others when he is in a position to do so.

After his retirement from the Springfield News–Sun, Allan will go on to inspire young writers through his work at Clark State College and at Wittenberg University. He and David will stay in touch until Allan's death in 2014. When David himself retires, he will call Allan and thank him for giving him a chance.

Together, this generation of Springfield newsmen will bring out the best in David, teaching him to search objectively and open-mindedly for the facts and the truth, to seek all viewpoints on any issue, to be skeptical about self-serving behavior, and never to underestimate the power of the published word.

They also show grace in how they handle his rookie mistakes, of which there will be several. From these mentors, David learns much, and applies it in his own career in the years to come.

David's next great professional mentor will be a brilliant, funny, creative newspaper editor just about the right age to be an older brother in the Workman family.

Ralph Langer will see possibilities in David that will startle the young journalist when he looks back on them from the vantage point of hindsight. David is 24 years old when the managing editor hires him for his second "big break" in newspapering.

He brings him to the Dayton Journal Herald, which in 1973 is a dynamic, exciting, challenging place to be a journalist. In doing so, Ralph reunites David with the newspaper that changed his life in 21 years earlier under when Chesta Fulmer published the "Letter from Alabama."

Ironically, when David happily accepts the offer to become a reporter for "The JH," he is just becoming aware that this was the newspaper that published Luella Smith's letter in 1952. In fact, at this point in his life, David has never seen the letter; he has only heard about it. Nor does he know Luella's name.

In Dayton, the 24-year-old journalist will be exposed to truly excellent writing and reporting and newspapering. The company established by the late Governor Cox has produced the likes of Erma Bombeck, who will become a nationally syndicated humor columnist; D.L. Stewart, a witty and hilarious columnist in the '70s and '80s; Pulitzer Prize winning cartoonist Mike Peters; and prolific historian Allan Eckert, who pioneered the art of meticulously researched, powerfully written narrative history. David will own many of Eckert's books, devouring every word.

One of the most senior staff members whom David works with remembers Journal Herald advice columnist Chesta Fulmer, with whom he worked until her death in 1957. He remembers her as a kind and thoughtful, and smart, woman. David will always regret that he could not personally thank her for publishing the letter that changed his life—the Letter from Alabama.

Soon after arriving at the Journal Herald, David is assigned to investigate consumer complaints about a supposed contractor who has defrauded innocent customers of many thousands of dollars intended for home improvements. For the writing of a series of articles about this consumer rip-off, David is paired up with a wonderful writer named Ann, or Annie, Heller. As David brings in the results of his investigation, Annie helps him write the articles in such a compelling yet factual way that they have real power, revealing the true impact of this fraud on the lives of real Daytonians. Under her guidance, a young reporter becomes also a writer.

When the contractor threatens David during a phone call, saying "if you print that, you won't live to see another sunrise," Managing Editor Ralph Langer immediately writes a letter to Dayton's police chief, with a copy to the threatening con man. The letters are hand-delivered that very day.

David duly and gratefully notes another life lesson. Quality leaders and quality organizations stand up for their people.

A couple of years later, David sees a group of colleagues gathered at the bulletin board of the Journal Herald newsroom. On it is posted a memo from Ralph. In an era when there is no such thing as email or social media, the best way to announce news that affects an entire work place is to post a paper memo on a cork bulletin board where everyone has the opportunity to see it at the same time.

Ralph's memo announces that he has accepted a job as

Editor of the daily newspaper in Everett, Washington, on the shores of Puget Sound, between the Olympic Mountain Range and the Cascade Mountain Range. It sounds heavenly to a young man who loves the outdoors.

Upon reading the memo, David walks right over to Ralph's managing editor's office and pokes his head in the door (Ralph's door is almost always open). Receiving the go-ahead to come in, David tells his mentor: "Congratulations, Ralph. I'm sorry to see you go."

He thanks his boss for taking a chance on him, and giving a great opportunity here at The JH.

Ralph mentions that he is hoping to be doing some hiring in Everett, Washington. David leaves no doubt he would love to work for Ralph again.

In May of 1976, 27-year-old David Workman and wife Bonnie board a commercial airliner for the first time, flying from Dayton to Seattle for an interview. To David's utter amazement, he is interviewing not for a job as a reporter, but city editor of a daily newspaper. This is the person who makes reporting assignments, who edits stories, and who helps conduct personnel evaluations for the newspaper. After a very challenging screening process, Herald Publisher Robert Best Jr. approves the hiring of David to be his newspaper's City Editor.

In Everett, David will have the life-altering experience of working one-on-one with a truly transformational leader. Ralph has an unsurpassed ability to motivate, inspire and support the very best work, and to achieve phenomenal results from a group.

Ralph is one of those leaders against whom people measure all of the other leaders in their lives. He brings out the very best in people and in an organization of people.

One busy morning, he steps out of his Editor's office, takes several steps to David's desk where the young city editor is busily—perhaps frantically—editing stories for today's afternoon paper.

Ralph says, "What can I do to help you?"

David assures his boss that he can handle it.

Ralph says, "But you're really busy and I'm not. Let me help you."

David hands his boss and mentor some copy to edit. Later, he will realize that, in that moment, he has learned the value of delegating. He will become better and better at letting more people help so that everyone succeeds in getting the work done. He learns it's not a sign of failure or weakness to get help when it's needed.

From Ralph Langer, David will learn many other skills of leadership. One of them that especially stands out is the skill of recognizing when a person is in the wrong job, but can make a big contribution in a different job. Learning from Ralph's example, David will employ this skill in the remaining three decades of his own career, to the benefit of everyone involved.

Ralph is also a visionary, seeing what could be if someone makes it so. Often this requires thinking big and, as some would say, "out of the box." It also requires the capacity for getting others to share your vision. Nobody does this better than Ralph Langer.

One of the ways Ralph creates a shared vision is to involve all the right people in the decision-making process. Instead of leaving people in the dark, he brings them into the room, gets their perspectives, and arrives at well-considered decisions. In a later era, some leadership gurus will call it "360-degree" decision-making—referring to the 360 degrees of the compass. For Ralph, it's just SOP—standard operating procedure. And it works.

In 1981, after the Best family has sold the Everett Herald, Ralph and David find themselves suddenly out of work. Ralph goes on to the Dallas Morning News as Managing Editor and then as Editor and Executive Vice President. He will lead Texas' premier newspaper to several Pulitzer Prizes for journalistic excellence.

David does not attempt to follow his mentor and friend to Dallas, but he will stay in close touch for the rest of their lives, and will put to good use the leadership lessons from Ralph.

Arlie Mills, Scoutmaster

Another of David's early mentors and role models is Arlie Mills.

At age 11, David crosses over from Cub Scout Pack 28 at Kenwood Heights Elementary School to Boy Scout Troop 73 at Trinity Lutheran Church on Sunset Avenue in Springfield. His first Scoutmaster there is Francis, a playful dad whose son is also in the troop. For a couple of years, he is the one who leads the boys on hikes, campouts, Scouting competitions, and such. From him, David learns camp craft skills such as roasting bread over a campfire in a form known as "twist on a stick." Francis drives an old Chevy sedan, and on the gas cap, he paints a bat on a background of silver paint. He calls it The Bat Mobile. The boys in the troop get a kick out of it.

Francis convinces his best buddy, Arlie Mills, who had once upon a time been a Scout with him, to join Troop 73 as Assistant Scoutmaster. This may just be the best recruiting move in the long and storied history of recruiting.

When Francis and his son leave Scouting, Arlie steps up to the plate. Although his son, Billy, is only a toddler—years from becoming a Scout—Arlie throws himself into his role as a leader and mentor of boys.

He is exactly what the Scouts of Troop 73 need. Exactly what Second Class Scout David Workman needs.

Arlie is really smart, as in . . . really smart. He is super cool without the slightest hint of pretense. The boys of Troop 73 will never pull the wool over Arlie's eyes, although they will try.

He is also a skilled craftsman who can make just about anything with his hands. On the job, he turns hunks of lifeless metal into precision tools and machines. Even more amazing is his skill at helping boys become men—and not just men, but men with a purpose in life.

Later on, Arlie will teach at the vocational school in Marion, Ohio. A question that he will ask his machine-shop students is: "What's your goal in life?" For Arlie, it isn't enough to graduate from school or earn badges in Scouting. The point is to have a vision and a plan for using what you learn, and then to start doing it.

As a Scoutmaster, Arlie opens doors to fun and adventures to last a lifetime. Through personal sacrifice and commitment, Arlie makes it possible for a bunch of boys from Springfield, Ohio, to dream impossible dreams—and, working together, to make their dreams come true.

With him, and thanks to him, the boys will have their first true wilderness experience—a week or more of paddling gear-laden canoes on beautiful, forested Algonquin lakes in the Canadian Shield region, where they will hear the unmistakable call of the loon and the haunting howl of the wolf. From a rocky promontory, the Scout leader and the Scouts take in the view. For 360 degrees, all they see is wildness—lakes, stream, forest and blue sky. It is magnificent.

During the days of long-distance paddling on big water, David and his canoe partner John Hursh realize they have become a single unit, stroking in unison and anticipating each other's next move with no verbal communication needed. It's as close to perfect rhythm as David will ever get.

David and his buddies don't realize it at the time, but Arlie is fostering confidence in themselves, in each other and their team. And fostering appreciation for the Creator of all things.

He gives them pride and confidence in their ability to hike, camp, administer first aid, paddle a canoe across big water, and cook for themselves on open fires before backpacking stoves or freeze-dried meals are available to them.

He makes sure they can tie useful (and previously mysterious) knots—which they will still be putting to use half a century later. Square knots, bowlines, two-half-hitches, clove hitches, taut-line hitches—these and many other twists of the rope will never intimidate David and his buddies because they were the Scouts of Troop 73.

On top of it all, David and many other boys will experience leadership, problem-solving, planning and follow-through to make big ideas turn into real-life adventures. Guided by Arlie's example and encouragement, they will not be intimidated when leadership is called for in their future lives.

Arlie and David will become lifelong friends, talking on the phone a few times a year. Arlie and wife Lois from Ohio will visit David's family in Olympia, Washington, and take a hike together in the wild and scenic Olympic National Park. In 2013, two years after Arlie's death, David and his wife, Clover, will stand with Lois at Arlie's gravesite in Iberia, Ohio. David will silently thank his mentor, friend, and leader of boys.

—16—
Best Pen Pal Ever

In the 21st century, when words fly back and forth continually on the Internet, when friends and family and casual acquaintances comment back and forth on social media about all manner of things, it takes some stretching to recall a time when it was not so.

Until the 1990s, physical distance is a barrier to communication. People who care about one another can lose touch with each another. People can seem to disappear. The only solutions to this are to make a phone call, on a land line—or to sit down, pen or pencil in hand, and write a note or a letter and affix a stamp to an envelope, and deposit it into a physical mailbox.

Before the advent of electronic and wireless communication, if people live far apart, phone calls have their limitations. First, there are long-distance charges, because there are no "family package" plans in the age of land lines. And until the 1980s, if no one answers at the other end of the phone line, you are out of luck. There is no voice messaging, not even recording of messages. These advances have not yet advanced.

David is lucky to have the best Pen Pal ever. Cynthia does not let 130 road miles separate them. Over the years of their childhood, it is quite possible that she will write hundreds of notes and letters to him.

The earliest one that he will rediscover in his adulthood dates from elementary school days. On lined paper, in careful cursive script, Cynthia writes a poem:

My Brother

My brother is so sweet,
He is so neat.
He has a good bongo beat.

(This line comes as a delightful surprise to the adult David when he reads it. No one else has ever accused him of having musical talent!)

> *My brother is also nice.*
> *He is filled with sugar and spice.*
> *He dose (sic) not have any lice.*

> *My brother doesn't pick fights with me.*
> *He never hurts a little bee.*
> *He is careful when he climbs a tree.*

(This last verse, he will later agree, is true.)

> *By Your Sister*

At the bottom of the page, she writes:
"P.S.

"Thought you would like it. I've got the mumps. I'll tell you about it in the letter."

The adult David smiles inside and out, upon reading this.

The accompanying letter, alas, does not find its way into David's lifelong collection of correspondence from Cynthia. But the poem does, because Mom and Dad have kept it. And when they have passed away, David will find it in the papers they deemed most valuable to them.

Sometime in the high school years, David begins saving the notes and letters from the sister he dearly loves.

They reveal a delightful sense of humor. She teases him about a condition that he seems to have that she calls "crampitis." This condition apparently explains why he doesn't write often enough to her.

The shoe box of correspondence also reflects the importance that friendships and relationships hold for Cynthia. She asks about friends that David has introduced her to on her many visits to Springfield. She also reports on her friends whom she has introduced David to during his many visits to Loudonville and Massillon.

It is apparent that Cynthia is paying attention to David's life and adventures. For example, in his senior year of high school, when he is procrastinating at applying for college scholarships, his kid sister doesn't hesitate to remind him, even nag him.

She inquires as whether he is staying in touch with their next-oldest brother, Jack, who is married and living in Springfield now and starting his family.

One beautiful effect of the boxful of sisterly correspondence is that the note and letters remind him of fun and adventures and double-dates that they have had together as teens. Without the letters, he would certainly have forgotten some of these shared experiences.

One letter, from late spring 1968, rings a bell in his distant memory. In it, Cynthia tells David about her fast-approaching graduation from Jackson Memorial High School near Massillon. She mentions a ring that she has been admiring.

Little does Cynthia know, at the time of her writing, that David has been conspiring with Gene and Mickey to surprise her on her graduation night. He will be getting off work early at the dairy, and will drive his all-black, only-slightly-rusty 1950 Pontiac sedan up the highway to Massillon. And the gift that he will be bringing her is the exact ring that she has been admiring.

The surprise works perfectly. She jumps up and down with excitement when her big brother drives the "black beast" Pontiac into the Workman driveway at Massillon.

The 330-mile round trip from Springfield to Massillon will be one to remember for another reason. On U.S. 30, not far from Cynthia's house, David is cruising along at 50 or so miles per hour when he begins hearing a rumbling from the tailpipe. Then he hears the sound of metal scraping on pavement. He pulls off the highway onto the shoulder, and then he notices an Ohio Highway Patrol trooper driving up.

The trooper walks up to the car, fixes his gaze on the 19-year-old behind the wheel of the ancient jalopy, and asks what the problem is. David explains the sounds he has just heard.

Said trooper gets down on his knees, looks under the car and sees the muffler hanging on the ground from a broken exhaust pipe.

The officer tugs on the muffler, freeing it from the car so that it doesn't become a road hazard.

He then describes the situation to a rather intimidated David, and asks when he can get the exhaust system replaced. David explains his predicament and his urgent need to be at his sister's graduation. The trooper—perhaps a father?—takes pity and writes David a warning ticket, saying the car cannot be driven any later than the following Monday unless the muffler and tailpipe are replaced.

A relieved David gladly takes the warning ticket and is, for the next couple of days, careful about accelerating in populated areas where the unmuffled roar of the Pontiac Straight Eight engine might not be appreciated.

Cynthia is amused by this story.

A year and a half later, she is married to her sweetheart, John Rohr. Six months after that, David is married to the young woman who, in time, will give birth to two beautiful baby girls who will become beautiful and remarkable women and mothers.

In April 1971, Cynthia types a letter to David that displays her good-natured teasing, and also her unbounded pride in him. Before dashing off to work this morning, she taps out a quick note. She has just seen an entertaining feature article he had written for the Springfield morning newspaper, which had been reprinted in other newspapers—including one in the Massillon area. Apparently, she encloses a clipping of the article, because she breezily instructs him to autograph it for her, and not to lose it, thank you.

Cynthia tells him she is "so darn happy, proud, and excited beyond belief."

When David re-reads this letter 43 years later, he is overwhelmed. It is the last note or letter that he would receive from the sister who is so much a part of him. Now, he is the one who is proud to be her flesh and her blood. Cynthia was the one who was wise, and deep, fragile and strong, and mature beyond her years.

In June 1971, just when it is beginning to look as if David and Cynthia and their spouses will be in a position to make plans together, she is hospitalized with complications from kidney disease that had been diagnosed in her first year of high school. Before the month is out, she is taken from those who love her.

David's children will never know Cynthia through their own experience. Nor will Mark's nor Carol's nor Cathy's nor Cheryl's children.

However, she will not be forgotten. The next generation of Workmans will have Cynthias, whose names will be inspired by her siblings' deep love for this extraordinary person who gave so much and was taken away too soon.

Sister and brother in Loudonville
on a special day

—17—
Revelations

Although he started life as a Laswell, David becomes a Workman through and through. In the process, no secrets are kept from him. Family members don't speak of George, his birth father, unless David asks, or unless there's another reason to do so. But whenever the subject comes up, all of David's questions are answered as best they can be.

Although he has no memory of George, David knows that his own name includes Laswell. His school report cards list him as David Lee Laswell Workman. The cards list Ralph and Louise Workman as his guardians. At age 21, the young man will go to the Clark County courthouse and legally become David Lee Workman.

From an early age, David hears the story from Ralph, Louise, and his sisters and brothers of how he disappeared for a time and how he was reunited with his family. He enjoys stories of his infancy and childhood. Each story, slowly over time, fills in a piece of his picture of how he started out in life.

Although David asks questions about his past from time to time, he almost never asks about George. He doesn't need George. He has a father, thank you. He has Dad.

Ralph is so thoroughly his dad, and Louise is so thoroughly his mom, that he doesn't grow up feeling like anything is missing in the parent department. His one regret is that he and Cynthia don't live together full-time, but as Cynthia wrote in her 1968 note, both of them gained two great families by living apart.

For most of his life, David avoids thinking of his birth father because he doesn't in any way want to be disloyal to his real father, Ralph. In truth, Ralph has never said or done anything to indicate that questions about George would strike him as disloyalty. It doesn't matter to David; he has one dad—Ralph. That's all he needs.

As the years pass, questions do come to David about other people in his life story. And as they arise, he asks them. He wonders about the woman in Alabama who kept him for several months. He has heard about the letter in the newspaper, and he asks about that. He wonders who saw the newspaper letter and contacted Granddad Workman—Ralph Sr. Unfortunately, little to nothing is known in the Workman family about these people.

David also begins to wonder about mother Hortense, although he hesitates to ask many questions. Perhaps he wants to avoid the possibility of hurting his mom's feelings. Louise removes any doubts he may have. When David is a father in his own right, she gives him a wonderful gift—a collage of photos showing David with BOTH of his mothers. There are sweet pictures of David with Louise. There is a tender photo of David being held in Hortense's arms as he wails his head off.

This photo set, which will hang on the walls of his home for decades, sets David free to ask about, and think about, Mother Hortense, while fiercely loving Mom, Louise.

If there is a day that marks the beginning of David's own personal journey into his past, it may be the day in 1973 when he visits the Dayton morning newspaper's microfilm archive for late May 1952. He eagerly turns the film reel back through the pages of time, searching for Chesta Fulmer's advice column. He finds the "Letter from Alabama."

For the first time in his life, David reads the actual words from Mrs. Carl G. Smith of Route 2, Box 80-E, Mobile, Alabama. He reads about George S. Laswell of Meeker Road, Dayton, leaving his little son with her.

David reads Chesta's response: "Dear Friend, I am sure this gentleman will contact you. Perhaps he is ill somewhere. I can well understand your worry, and hope that you get good news."

David, the young adult, is filled with feelings that defy words. He prints out a copy on the heat-sensitive paper that the microfilm reader is equipped with. He takes the print-out with him. Although it will fade and become illegible in a few years, it is the first tangible record that he has of a time in his life that he cannot remember.

As he reads and re-reads the Letter from Alabama, he is filled with wonder and gratitude that Mrs. Carl G. Smith kept him safe and returned him to his family. And he feels a need to say two simple words: "Thank you."

And so, one Saturday morning in 1973, David takes in hand the telephone that hangs on the wall of his kitchen. He dials 555-1212, and the Bell Telephone operator says: "Directory Assistance. What city, please?"[xix]

David replies: "Mobile, Alabama."

After being connected with an operator 700 miles away on Gulf Coast, David asks for the number for Carl G. Smith. There are several possible Carl Smiths, so David picks the first one, and gets the number. Then he calls it.

In no time at all, David is speaking with Mr. Carl Smith, and gives the briefest possible explanation of who he is and why he is calling. He wonders: "Is this the right Carl Smith?"

The man at the other end says: "I'm Carl G. Smith Jr." And he explains that his father passed away nearly thirty years earlier, and it was his mother who wrote the Letter from Alabama. She, too, passed away several years earlier.

Carl remembers David. He adds, very kindly: "We weren't trying to get rid of you. We thought your family would be worried and would want you back."

And David says, "I just want to thank you. I have a great life. I am very grateful to your mother and your family."

The conversation is brief, just a few minutes. But as a young man, he has said words that he never imagined himself saying, to a man who is a perfect stranger. A perfect stranger whose family helped to save him.

At the time, David does not recognize the improbability of his connecting so easily with the son of Luella Smith. It will later be revealed that Carl Jr. was a long-haul trucker, spending only a few waking hours of each week at home. David has called Luella's son at the right hour on the right day.

Thirty-seven years later, an older David, who is now a father and grandfather, will yearn for more information about the woman who took care of him for six months after George left him in Alabama.

At this point in time, finding people is much easier—if they are still living. On the Internet, using a couple of search engines, he learns more about Luella Smith, widow of Carl G. Smith Sr. and mother of Carl G. Smith Jr.

On a genealogy web page in the summer of 2010, David reads about Luella and Carl Sr., and he is able to contact the author, a retired public relations professional living in Virginia. This man connects him with a younger cousin, Carl Smith in Mobile, Alabama.

Carl is the grandson of Luella. He is the son of Carl Jr., whom David had talked on the phone with in 1973.

David and this Carl learn about each other for the first time.

Carl, it turns out, was a teenager when his grandmother passed away in 1963. He remembers her place out in the country—a location that, in 2010, is no longer out in the country. Carl remembers the drive to the house on the narrow road bordered by drainage ditches.

Since those years, Carl has become a father and grandfather and will retire after a career on the oil rigs in the Gulf of Mexico.

David at this time is a couple of years from retiring after a career in communication. He instinctively likes Luella's grandson Carl, and they stay in touch, talking on the phone from time to time. They become Facebook friends and follow one another's families from 2,100 miles apart.

Carl graciously provides photos of his grandparents, including an exterior of the home where David spent six crucial months of his young life. For the first time, David can see with his own eyes what his childhood memory had lost sight of.

David can't help but think that his dad and mothers, Ralph and Louise and Hortense, would be very pleased.

And maybe Luella would be, too.

—18—
A Writer Is Born

The oldest record of David's efforts at creative writing is dated March 1960 when he is a fifth-grader. Completing a Language assignment, he pulls out a sheet of lined paper and a No. 2 graphite pencil, and in a neat and careful cursive style that he can only admire (and not imitate) in later years, he writes a very short story:

> *One time a cornstalk that was standing in a field grew until it reached the sun. The heat of the sun made the corn pop. A mule standing in the field thought it was a snow storm in June, so he lay down in it and froze to death. That was the end of that little mule!*

It will not win prizes, except one. It will be prized by Louise and Ralph Workman. They will save it, and keep it, for him to find in their papers in 1996.

David's life as a writer takes a giant step forward when he makes the pivotal decision to enroll in the typing class at South High.

In the 1960s, the best—that is, the fastest and most accurate—typists in Springfield, Ohio, are not male. Typing requires mastering a bewildering jumble of flat keys attached to thin steel arms that drive the type bars onto sheets of paper on big, bulky, clunky machines called manual typewriters.

Most of the kids taking the class are planning to become typists or secretaries. David wants to write school papers faster. And it doesn't hurt that there are cute girls in the class.

Soon, this decision pays off. Instead of laboriously writing school reports and term papers in long-hand cursive, David finds he can dramatically shorten the amount of time each written product takes by typing each one.

He discovers that he has to "think differently" when composing a school paper on a typewriter. Within a few weeks, his brain transforms how it processes the words that flow through his head and out his finger tips. He will never again find it easier to think-and-write in long-hand. From here on out, he is a think-and-type writer.

Little does he know that becoming a touch-typist will transform his life and work. The ability to type and compose on a manual typewriter will prove to be as life-changing as, one day, writing on a computer will be.

David's first mentors in the newspaper business will be men who never learned to touch-type. They will be "hunt and peck" typists. This means their eyes seek out each key before their fingers touch it. They will be super-fast at hunting and pecking, but their eyes must always be on the keys.

By contrast, a touch-typist has memorized the keys, and the fingers naturally find their way to each key while the typist-writer's eye is fixed on the subject matter, not on the keys.

In his senior year, David puts his new typing-writing skills to use on the pages of the South High School Herald. After graduating from high school, he will put these skills to work as a student at the newly minted Wright State University—one of a host of college campuses that spring up to educate the early wave of Baby Boomers.

While David begins his college studies, he remembers Mrs. Wolf's confidence in him that he could make a living as a newspaper writer and editor.

So he begins to search for a job as a paid journalist. College, after all, is expensive. Tuition at Wright State is $490 per year. That's a lot of Indian Head Pennies. And it doesn't include books! At prices like this, David's savings from his River Dale Dairy paychecks won't last long.

Mrs. Wolf and Mary Jane Schreiber (mother of friend Lisa Schreiber, and the editor of the "society" pages at the Springfield newspapers) go to bat for him by putting in a good word for him at the News and Sun. Between the two of them, they manage to get David an informational interview with Loren Schultz, the managing editor of the morning and afternoon newspapers in Springfield.

Mr. Schultz seems interested in David, but receiving no strong signal that he will soon be on the payroll of Cox Newspapers in Springfield, Ohio, David turns his sights to the local radio station, WBLY—known to Springfielders as 'Wobbly.'

Nineteen-year-old college freshman David Workman makes an appointment to visit the manager of the station. On the appointed day, David arrives early. It's important to be punctual, and this job-seeker is taking no chances of being late.

After presenting himself at the front desk of WBLY, David is invited to sit and wait for his appointment. In time, David is sitting in the manager's office, explaining that he wants to be a radio broadcaster.

The manager smiles pleasantly at the 19-year-old, and explains: "Well, Dave, if you want to be a broadcaster, you have to have a Third-Class Radiotelephone Operators License with a broadcast endorsement from the Federal Communications Commission."

"Oh," replies David. "How do I get one of those?"

The manager explains the process of studying for such license, and then driving to Columbus—the state capital—and taking the test at the office of the FCC.

"Thank you for meeting with me," David says. As the student walks through the door onto the street outside, his mind is immediately working on the question of how soon he can obtain a Third Class Radiotelephone Operator's License with a broadcast endorsement so he can go to work for WBLY.

He calls Directory Assistance and obtains the number for the FCC office in Columbus. In the late 1960s, voice mail has not been invented. At least not in Central Ohio. When you call a business or government office during business hours, someone answers the phone, and you speak to that someone. David asks to receive a copy of the study booklet for a Third Class Radiotelephone Operator's License from the FCC.

Soon, David has received the study booklet, has memorized to his satisfaction the pertinent information, and has scheduled his test in Columbus at the office of the Federal

Communications Commission. In short order, David proudly receives in the United States Mail his Third Class Radiotelephone Operator's License with a broadcast endorsement. It is now legal for him to talk into a microphone on the public airwaves of the United States of America.

America's newest radio man can hardly wait to get a follow-up appointment at WBLY. Soon, he presents himself once again at the radio station office, and eagerly informs the man behind the desk that he is ready to go to work as a radio broadcaster.

The man behind the desk smiles pleasantly, pauses, and pops a question: Does America's newest radio man happen to have a sound check tape?

A what?

A sound check tape.

You, see, a radio station needs to know how a future broadcaster sounds when speaking on air.

"Well, no, I don't have a tape. How do I get one?"

The man behind the desk says David can go into an adjoining room and do a taped sound test right here at the station.

"That would be great," says America's newest radio man.

David enters the recording room, blurts out something that is duly taped, and he then inquires as to when he should expect to hear about the results of the taping.

David is informed that they will listen to the tape and let him know if they have any openings for a new broadcaster. That is the last that David will ever hear from WBLY. On the positive side, his Third Class Radiotelephone Operator's License will occupy a special place in a wooden chest for decades to come. Eventually, it will accompany him to several homes in two states.

Soon enough, David accepts the idea that he will not have a broadcasting career on the radio. Ever the optimist, however, and needing a job that will help pay for college, David discovers that Springfield will soon have its own television station.

This is big news!

In the 1960s, television programming in America consists of signals that are broadcast over the public airwaves between signal-sending towers and signal-receiving antennas. At the Workman home on Beacon Street in Springfield, the TV set occupies the prime space in the living room. All chairs, and the couch, are situated within sight of the TV set, which is a boxy piece of furniture filled with tubes and wires. The TV set stands about three feet high on the floor in front of the stairway that leads upstairs. It measures maybe 30 inches wide by 30 inches deep. Outside the house stands a tower topped with a TV antenna, which hauls in the signals and feeds them into the box of tubes.

All eyes are focused on the TV when it is turned on.

In Springfield, TV sets receive signals from a few broadcast stations that are all affiliated with a major national network—CBS, NBC and ABC. These signals bring programming that is visible on one of a few VHF (Very High Frequency) channels, such 2, 4, 6. These stations are located in the bigger cities of the region—Dayton, Columbus and Cincinnati.

However, in 1968, Springfield is supposed have its very own local programming, on Channel 26, a UHF (Ultra-High Frequency) channel.

For David, this is exciting stuff. Channel 26 will need to hire people, not only to present news and other information on the air, but also to write "copy" such as program content and advertising.

By now, David has accepted the idea that he won't be an on-air broadcast personality. The sound check tape at WBLY settled that for him.

So he makes an appointment at Channel 26, to apply for the job of writing commercials. He goes to the Wright State University library and finds a book that gives some examples of broadcast ad writing. He studies it. He practices writing commercials. On the typewriter, of course.

He presents himself at the new local TV station, and is given a test on writing TV commercials. As he leaves, he is pretty confident that he aced the test. For weeks, David awaits the call offering him a commercial-writing job at Channel 26. Eventually, he accepts the cold reality that Channel 26 does not need his writing skills. He is pretty down-in-the-mouth for the weeks leading up to the big day when Channel 26 debuts on the air.

David and his parents turn on the TV that big day, and switch the dial to "26." To their eyes, it all looks pretty amateurish, not at all like the well-established big-city broadcast stations in Dayton, Columbus and Cincinnati. And as for the commercials, well, there aren't many. There are gaps in programming when the screen is absolutely blank.

After watching Channel 26 for a while, Ralph turns to David: "Well, son, it looks like that is the best job that you never got."

That bit of ironic humor is the perfect antidote for David's down-in-the-dumps mood. Never again will he give any thought at all to becoming a broadcaster. In a couple of years, Channel 26 will go off the air.

On the last week of October 1968, David is watching his future brother-in-law, little Michael, try on his trick-or-treat costume when Ralph or Louise calls with the news that Mr. Loren Schultz has called him.

Bingo!

At last, he has a job at a newspaper. He will work one or two nights per week in the sports department of the morning paper, The Sun—that same paper that he had delivered to porches around his part of town. The job involves taking scores over the phone from high school athletic teams in outlying locations of the newspaper's service area, and then writing a couple of paragraphs on each contest.

First, however, his services are needed on presidential election night 1968. His job will be standing watch in the teletype room of the newspaper, amid the clacking of the "wire" machines that haul in Associated Press reports from around the nation and world.

David drives downtown, parks his light-blue 1963 Chevy Biscayne, and walks through the imposing doors of the Italian Renaissance Revival style News and Sun Building. He walks through the expansive lobby past the switchboard and front desk, up the broad staircase, past the second-floor executive offices, on to the third-floor news room.

There he encounters a room full of desks, each assigned to a different reporter or editor. In the background is the clattering sound of the teletype room, tat-tat-tatting today's news from all around the world.

The Sun's newest newsroom employee is assigned the job of monitoring election updates as they unspool off the teletype, ripping the copy paper off the machine, then taking each piece of paper a few feet to the editors who are collecting all the news and making decisions about what will be published in the morning paper. It's exciting for the college sophomore to watch the election news coming into his very own hands.

In 1968, any words that are published in the newspaper must go through a tortuous process: first, someone types them up; then someone edits them with a pencil; then the piece of paper with the pencil edits goes to someone who is operating a Linotype machine, who re-types the words, which are then spat out as lines of lead type; then the lines are locked into place in a page form; then the page of type is inked and a "page proof" is made; and an editor reviews the proof for errors. Eventually, after more steps, the words will fly off a massive two-story-tall printing press in the day's newspaper.

David's role in getting the November 6, 1968, Springfield morning newspaper out is minuscule, but he is energized to be a part of it.

Early the next morning when David crawls into bed at the house on Beacon Street, the presidential race is still too close to call. It will be a few hours before Richard Nixon gives his victory speech and Hubert Humphrey gives his concession.

The spoiler in this race is George Wallace, a segregationist former (and future) governor of Alabama.

On a Friday soon after the election, newspaperman David returns to the News and Sun Building, re-ascends the staircase, and re-enters the newsroom. Here, he is introduced to the men in the sports department at the far right side of the big, wide-open news room, which is filled with metallic office desks and chairs—row after row of them.

He will learn that James "Scotty" Reston, famed New York Times journalist, got his start right here in this same newsroom in the 1930s. Sports Editor Dan Hoyt, a genial and kindly man, remembers young Scotty.

Tonight, David will begin to learn the job of gathering and reporting the news. He is temporarily assigned to one of the metallic desks with a phone sitting on it and with a clanky manual typewriter resting at just the right height for efficient typing.

After tonight's high school games are over, the phones begin to ring. David takes a phone call from a scorekeeper who has witnessed and recorded the basic facts about one of the games played by high schools in outlying communities.

The newly minted sports writer in the Sun newsroom cradles the phone "receiver" on his shoulder. He inserts two pieces of letter-size paper (not stationery paper, but basic old newsprint paper, cut to size), with a sheet of carbon paper sandwiched in between, into the typewriter. He turns the roller, adjusting the copy paper so it's ready for action. As the scorekeeper dictates the information, David taps away at the keys on the machine. Each time the typewriter carriage reaches the end of its run, David hits the carriage return bar with his right hand. This sends the carriage, with its two pieces of newsprint and single sheet of carbon paper, flying back to the left side of the typewriter.

At this moment, David is very thankful for his touch-typing class at South High School.

His first published story as a cub reporter isn't exactly electrifying: The Yellow Springs Bulldogs defeat the Bethel Bees in their opening basketball game of their season. However, the story is important enough that Ralph or Louise will clip it out of the morning newspaper, and put it in a special envelope, where David will find it three decades later.

As the weeks pass, David will be called on to work more hours—about 20 per week—taking information over the phone from local funeral homes and writing the obituaries that will testify to the lives and deaths of hundreds of people in and around Springfield and Clark County, Ohio. In January 1969, he is reporting on the labor dispute at Wright State University, where he is a sophomore. From this point, he is off and running as a journalist.

Over the next 20½ years, David will be lucky enough to make a good living as a newspaper writer, reporter and editor in Ohio and in Washington State, followed by 23½ years as a communicator and educator in state service. In the process, he will meet and know a lot of interesting people, and learn a lot about government, the justice system, human nature, and about con artists who prey upon innocent victims.

He will remember with special fondness speaking with, and writing about, many of these people. One day in the early 1970s, David's editor at the Springfield Sun gives him the assignment to drive over the Dayton to a hotel where he will meet a publicity agent and an American icon—silent-film star Lillian Gish. He will interview her and write a feature story.

This is not investigative reporting. Awards and recognition do not spring from such articles. However, David finds himself genuinely interested in people and their lives—their stories.

Few had more interesting lives than Miss Gish, who was born in 1893 in Springfield, in a neighborhood past which David used to walk on his way to South High School before he acquired his first car, a 1950 Nash Statesman.

Lillian's younger sister, Dorothy, was born in Dayton in 1898 and had passed away in 1968. Both had highly successful film careers, working initially for legendary filmmaker D.W. Griffith.

At the time of their interview, 20-something David Workman admires Lillian as a remarkable woman from humble Springfield beginnings who has accomplished so much and who continues to work at it into her old age. She is, after all, in her seventies.

Later, as 70 begins to look young to David, he realizes that Miss Lillian Gish, at the time of their interview, would have another 10 or 15 years of acting roles ahead of her. She would die at age 99 in 1993.

Biographies of the Gish sisters' lives would describe their father as undependable and mostly absent from the family. Their mother would be described as the primary provider for the family. Learning this gives David even more appreciation for two American legends.

If David has ever met someone with a more interesting life than Miss Gish, that person would be Isabel Arcasa, whom he meets in 1988 while researching and writing a series of articles for the newspaper in Tacoma, Washington. Just in time for the upcoming 1989 statehood centennial, his articles are published as a "Centennial Portrait" of the state and its people.

On a hot, blue-sky summer day, David Workman and Morning News Tribune photographer Bruce Larson find Isabel in the little town of Nespelem in the dry region of northeastern Washington State, where she lives on the 2,100-square-mile reservation of the Colville Confederated Tribes.

At the time, she is 98 years old—the most elder and therefore honored of the tribal members. She was born a year after Washington Territory became Washington State. She is the daughter of a Wenatchee Indian mother and a white settler. In her long life, she will intimately know two vastly different cultures.

In her lifetime, she acquires many names. As a girl, she has names that translate into English as Little Girl and as Sitting-in-a-Creek. In old age, the children of Nespelem call her Grandma or Auntie Bell. Her name in white culture is Isabel.

As a young girl, she saw the famed Chief Joseph of the Nez Perce, one of the tribes consigned to live on the Colville reservation. In Joseph's case, he was essentially a captive here of the United States government.

Although Isabel would drive a car until age 94, she didn't have her first ride in one until her 30s. As a girl and as a young woman, she rode horses across the dry Columbia Plateau landscape of eastern Washington and adjacent states.

In her 30s, she moved away from Nespelem to live and work in the white man's world—as wife of a farmer, as a Boeing employee, as a waitress and cook, and as a seamstress.

When David and Bruce meet her, Isabel expresses some regrets about the changes she has witnessed in her near century of life. Now that the people have cars, she says sadly, "we hardly even see each other." No longer do they travel by horse, stopping to spend time with kinsmen and to keep alive ancient traditions, she explains.

Another regret is the loss of the home ground where she spent her childhood. The place on the mighty Columbia River, called Whitestone for the big rock nearby, was submerged by the damming of the Columbia at Grand Coulee to create the massive reservoir known as Lake Roosevelt.

For the next four decades of David's life, the time spent getting to know Isabel / Little Girl / Sitting-in-a-Creek / Grandma / Auntie Bell will remain a highlight. He will always be thankful that he had the chance to paint a word portrait of a state and its people, especially this special American.

At the very beginning of David's writing career, in Springfield, he befriends a man named Harry whom he has met in the storefront campaign office of the Teen Age Republicans in 1968. The storefront was next to the bus stop that Harry and other senior citizens used when coming and going between their nursing home and downtown Springfield.

Over a two-and-a-half-year period, David visits Harry many times at his picturesque, spacious apartment at a local retirement home. They strike up a genuine friendship. David is entertained and amazed by Harry's gift for training the local squirrels. During his regular walks outside, the furry long-tailed rodents willingly scamper up his trouser leg, dive into his front pocket, retrieve peanuts, then scamper back down his trousers to extract the peanuts from their shells. David will never try this trick himself.

The younger man enjoys Harry's stories of a lifetime of experiences and memories. The two of them share an interest in history, and Harry is especially well-versed in the life of Abraham Lincoln. In time, he gives David some of his prized historical artifacts, including a cast-metal bust of Honest Abe fashioned immediately after the President's assassination.

"Dave," the older gentleman says one day in his apartment, which was built in the previous century, "I want you to have these things because you will care about them." His own family members, he says, aren't so interested in historical figures. David will treasure them.

One winter day, the younger man makes one of his visits at the retirement home to visit Harry, and discovers his elderly friend isn't in his usual room. The attendants direct him to a waiting room where he asks for Harry—who has been committed to the psychiatric ward.

Eventually, Harry comes out through the interior door. He is, quite simply, a shell of himself. No longer dressed in his own clothes, he is wearing a patient's garb. His face is pale; his eyes are sunken and lack their sparkle. In a hoarse voice, Harry whispers: "Dave, they are trying to kill me. They're drugging me."

David is shocked at these words. He doesn't know what to do for him. So after leaving his friend, the young man calls Harry's family in another part of Ohio and explains what he has seen and heard.

David will hear vastly different stories about why Harry was committed to the psych ward.

One thing is certain, however. He will never see Harry again alive. Before the young man can return for another visit, Harry will be dead. He will not make it to his 81st birthday.

Thirty years later, Harry will be on David's mind when he leads a team of professionals in Washington State government who will create a toll-free hotline that anyone can call, in virtually any language, any hour of the day or night, to report suspicions of abuse or neglect or exploitation of a vulnerable adult—or suspected abuse or neglect of a child—anywhere within Washington State.

In doing so, David will pay his everlasting respect, and love, to Harry.

Several years after Harry's death, and 2,400 miles away, David's work will introduce him to someone who will provide the opportunity to "pay forward" the good that strangers have done for him.

It happens in 1977, when David is on deadline at the newspaper in Everett, Washington, just north of Seattle. At the Everett Herald, David is the 28-year-old city editor—the person responsible for supervising the work of the newspaper's staff of local news reporters, and for editing local news articles before they are published each day.

On this particular morning, David is at his desk, which faces large windows overlooking Everett's Puget Sound harbor and the distant peaks of the rugged and beautiful Olympic Range, soon to be covered with winter white.

The young newspaperman's phone rings. At this time, there are no cellular or other mobile phones. David's only business phone is sitting on the desk in front of him. At the ring, he picks it up. Otherwise, it will continue to ring until someone answers it. This is how phone technology works in 1977.

At the other end of the line—yes, phone conversations are transmitted entirely by land lines at this time—a woman introduces herself as Shary. She has a problem, and she wonders if someone at the newspaper can help.

Shary is looking for the daughter she hasn't seen, or heard about, for seven years. She tells a heart-rending story of having lost contact with her three-year-old daughter after she and her husband divorced and the ex-husband remarried.

Now, seven years later, she has a glimmer of hope. A friend recently saw a name in a newspaper in another town. The name belongs to the woman who had married her former husband. Shary is wondering—desperately hoping, really—whether there is some way she might locate an address or phone number for the woman. Maybe, she hopes, the woman will help Shary find her now 10-year-old daughter. Shary pins her newfound hopes on the fact that the recent newspaper article makes it clear that her ex-husband is no longer married to the woman.

In the 21st century it's easy to forget there was a time, not so long ago, when locating a person in a distant city was not a simple matter of typing a name into an Internet search engine. In 1977, the best that most people might hope for is to be able to dial 555-1212 and get telephone Directory Assistance in a particular town. If you're lucky, the person you are trying to find has a "listed" phone number. If not, you have more work to do.

When Shary calls the newspaper office in her new home town, Everett, she cannot find a phone number or an address for the woman who had married and divorced Shary's ex-husband. Can the newspaper help her?

David takes a few minutes away from today's newspaper work to describe some of the tools that newspaper reporters use when they need to locate someone. One of them is called the "city directory." David explains: if the person you are looking for lives within the municipal boundary of a city, there's a good chance you can find a listing for the person in the local city directory.

"Where do I find a city directory?" Shary asks.

"Public libraries often have them for cities in the surrounding area," says the young newspaperman.

Armed with this information, Shary realizes that she doesn't need to find her ex-husband's ex-wife. She can skip the ex-wife and look for him. She thanks the newspaperman for his help, and they both hang up their telephone "receivers." She heads down to Everett's public library.

A few days later, Shary calls David at the Herald again. She gives him the news. She has located her ex-husband, and he said he would be happy to reunite her with their daughter.

Soon, Shary and her 10-year-old are together for the first time in seven years. In a few weeks, the entire family agrees to allow the Herald to publish their story—including a photo of a radiant mother with her arms around her beautiful, smiling daughter.

That photo—and the knowledge that a phone call to a newspaper office reunited a child with her mother—gives David an inner peace. He has partly repaid the invisible network of strangers who reunited him with his family through the pages of a newspaper in Dayton, Ohio, 25 years earlier.

It is the least that he could do.

Former Springfield South High School, now an innovative technology academy, 2010 photo courtesy of Cindy Funk

Photographic copy of 1920s postcard, Springfield News and Sun Building, courtesy of Nicholas Szempruch

—19—
Fatherhood

Over the course of David's life, two events will stand out in shaping him into the person he will become. First is Ralph Workman Jr.'s trip to Alabama in May 1952 to bring David home as a member of Ralph's and Louise's family. And, by extension, as a member of Gene and Mickey Workman's family.

Second is the November day two decades later when he becomes, for the first time, a parent.

The instant when he looks deeply into newborn Kara Elisabeth's eyes will change him into a new person. Now, in his 20s, he knows what it means to value someone else's life above his own. He discovers what it means to be on the giving end of unconditional love.

Later, it will happen again when he holds little Kirsten Cynthia in his arms. Still later, Kirsten will win his heart with "butterfly kisses" from her fluttering eyelashes.

He will take joy from the most ordinary things—such as trimming their tiny finger and toe nails, giving them baths, even replacing their stinky diapers and cleaning their little bottoms.

David will be won over by their giggles and grunts, their first words, their crawling, their first steps. He will become attuned to the sounds of their various cries, knowing which ones need attention and which ones need to be tolerated until they fall asleep.

He will love being a partner in parenting and in life with their mother.

One Father's Day, when the girls are young, Kara gives him a gift—a little tripod just the right size to stand on a desk or file cabinet top. And that is where it will be for decades to come. On it are these words:

God blessed me twice when he gave me you
He gave me a Dad and a great friend, too!

In all of this, David doesn't think about "making up for" having been abandoned by a birth father. To the contrary, his conscious thinking about parenthood springs from his memories and experiences with Ralph and Louise, his dad and his mom, and with Gene and Mickey and their children.

One night, however, a dark shadow of the distant past creeps into his consciousness. On this night, he wakes up in a cold sweat. Baby Kara is in the crib, sleeping quietly. Bonnie, an exhausted new mother, is asleep next to him. Everything is exactly as it should be.

However, he is seized by a horrible thought: "What if I die before Kara knows her father?"

He so desperately wants Kara to know her father. Not for himself. For her. He wants her to know that she is loved and that she is more precious than his own life.

Over the next few years, on random occasions, this fear will momentarily grip him. At these moments, the thought of dying before his daughters know their father nags at him until he banishes the thought from his head.

Then, around the time that Kirsten is four years old and Kara is nine, another thought washes over him: "If I should die now, Kara and Kirsten will know their father. I will not be a blank place in their lives." With the realization comes freedom. Freedom from a deep worry.

Proud and happy dad with Kirsten and Kara
on Easter Sunday

—20—
And What About George?

For sixty years of his life, David wouldn't think much, or often, about George Laswell. He doesn't hate him. He doesn't harbor regrets about his birth father. To the contrary, he feels a profound gratitude for how things turned out in his life—thanks to many people, including strangers.

After a lifetime of observing how some absentee parents have a way of boomeranging in and out of their children's lives, David is thankful that George didn't do that. Thankful that George didn't come back after he disappeared.

George Laswell basically doesn't exist for the son he left behind.

David had spent a life as a Workman and as a descendant of Hortense's Alsatian immigrant grandparents and great-parents. This was enough. He was the father of daughters and sons-in-law who are making the world better. What more could he possibly want?

If he opened himself up to thoughts about George, what else would he open himself up to? He was contented not to know.

Two things happened that would penetrate the wall around the non-father who left David in Alabama.

First, in 2002, David came into possession of a letter from George Laswell, sent to Gene Workman in Loudonville on April 18, 1961. The return address is General Delivery, San Diego, California. Years later, David will realize that, during this same time, George's nephew was stationed in San Diego when not at sea with the Navy. [xx] Whether that was more than a coincidence on George's part, David could only speculate.

George's two-page, typed letter crossed the continent, powered by a four-cent stamp bearing the profile of Abraham Lincoln, at a time when David was 12 years old and growing up in Springfield.

When Gene received this letter, he was a devoted husband father, and a respected member of the Loudonville community.

From San Diego, George had written him:

"This will be a difficult letter and yet it's one that I begin with far more freedom of will than I could ever have thought possible;

"First of all, Gene, this is not a letter requesting forgiveness even though I can hope that you too have come to know my Savior as intimately as has been my experience; in that way alone is there any possibility that you might find it possible to make any sort of allowance for what I have done for all concerned.

"Ommittance (sic) of names from this letter is done purposely because I can only hope that many of you have supposed me dead; and I might add that unless there is something of concrete good I can do in the future, it may be just as well that I remain so. You folks must determine that! As for any material worth I can ever be, only the future may answer; so far, all that I've managed to do is soil all I've touched and of course have broken my own heart in the process .
. . .

"Gene, it is not necessary for me to tell you what sort of man I was before your mother's death. I was far from perfect but that I was honorable AND IF I KNOW ANYTHING ABOUT MYSELF, I was happy and in love with our lives. WHAT MADE THIS CHANGE? You'll find the answer in the Bible: II Peter 2:20-22 . . . .

"Yes, I was for years a church member and before I was in the Army, a very active one but there came a time when, in the face of temptation, I fell. Because there was so little Spiritual understanding I didn't realize my deep need, so for several years I was satisfied to go to church when it was convenient to go but I made it a point to not allow myself to think very seriously about any-thing Spiritual.

"You know about my drinking habits up to the time of your mother's death. (I guess I was really drinking more than I wanted to admit but, even so alcohol was not a serious problem.) I don't know whether things would have been different if I had stayed in

Loudonville instead of going to Dayton to work; one thing sure, going to Dayton brought things to a climax. As you may well remember, I had another weakness which was probably as serious as drinking; in Dayton I sold out to both weaknesses and my downfall was speedy.

"If anyone had ever told me that I would actually desert my own son, I would have told him he was crazy; but it happened!!!

"Certainly, it would be a simple matter for you folks to deal with me through the law and I have now reached a point where I should be willing to return to Ohio to further simplify it if I thought it would do anybody any good. I fear tho' it could do nothing more than reopen old wounds and of course hurt some little guys who can remember little or nothing of those days.

"The one thing I'd like to do more than any-thing might be just as hurtful AND I'm not sure how much or how consistently I could supply money. During the past few months I have made next to nothing and I wonder how long it will be before any notable change will take place.

"My primary concern is that they know while they are still young that in all probability that alcohol will be pure poison to them. There are those people who should never touch any intoxicants; I was one, and in all probability it would be just as dangerous to them, please for their sakes get the message across to them. Of course, over and above that I am praying that there will be complete surrender of their lives to their God and Maker.

"I wish I could express on paper what you and Jack meant to me but in the face of what took place I think any-thing I would say would be absurd.

"May God bless you, is my prayer."

And in his own hand, he signed it, with an abbreviation:

"Geo. Laswell"

When David read the words from George—two pages that constitute the sum total of what the son will ever know about his birth father's thinking—he had conflicting feelings.

On the one hand, he was put off by the preachiness towards one of the Godliest people David has ever known—his brother Gene. On the other, he saw the signs of a man taking a degree of responsibility in a 12-step program of recovery.

Over time, this letter from the distant past began to chip away at the barrier that, for so long, had walled off thoughts of George within his former son.

Eight years later, just before Memorial Day in 2010, David and his wife Clover were having a late-night discussion about George. She was aware that her husband avoided seeking out information about the father who had abandoned him. She knew her husband had kept thoughts about George behind a locked door where they couldn't harm him or the people he loves.

Clover looked at her husband with compassion. "I can understand why you could be reluctant to find out more about your father," she said, then paused. "But if I were in your situation, I think I would want to know his story. I would want to know as much as I could about his life, because his story is a part of your story."

The words hung there in the air. David was thinking about them. They sank in, touching something deep.

Turning to his computer, David started his journey of discovery. It's a journey that would unravel some mysteries and, perhaps more importantly, connect David—and his children—with a part of him that had always been an empty mystery.

With computer mouse in hand, David clicked away, and opened a search engine on his computer. He typed in "George Shelton Laswell." Seconds later, he got the answer to a question that had long eluded him.

Turning to the woman who is his partner in life, he said: "George is dead."

The Internet revealed that George had died in 1966, and been buried in the Golden Gate National Cemetery south of San Francisco.

With this knowledge, David was freed to discover things previously unknown about himself, and to seek to know and better understand George Laswell's story.

Now the skills that he had acquired in a career as researcher and fact-finder went to work for him in his own personal quest. The Internet would yield troves of information about George's Laswell family—David's family.

Soon, David traced those Kentucky Laswells back to a likely connection with William Lasswell, who immigrated to colonial America from England in 1664.

He quickly learned a surprising amount about George's immediate family. It was partly inspiring, and partly tragic. None of it alarmed or intimidated him. To the contrary, George's parents and siblings were upstanding citizens. Late in life, his siblings would come together for large family reunions, posing in group photos and sharing their lives and life stories. [xxi]

In the process of discovering, David gained a first cousin whom he truly likes and admires. While the cousins may never have the opportunity meet in person, they struck up a mutually rewarding relationship made possible by modern long-distance communication. Rev. Sam Laswell, who is several years older, has lived most of his life in Michigan, is a veteran of the United States Air Force, is a retired Presbyterian pastor, and has written and studied a great deal about the Laswell and associated families.

Sam's deceased father, Wallis Haskew Laswell, was a son of Dr. Laswell and his second wife, Eunice Parker Ball Laswell. Sam willingly shares family knowledge, and David loves the signature blocks on his emails. "Grace to you and peace," Sam writes. And he concludes with meaningful quotations such as this from Lutheran theologian Dietrich Bonhoeffer, a martyr who was executed by the Nazis after a long imprisonment: "In ordinary life we hardly realize that we receive a great deal more than we give, and that it is only with gratitude that life becomes rich." Exactly.

George's father, Dr. William David Laswell, grew up in rural Kentucky near the Wilderness Road that the early settlers from Virginia and North Carolina followed through the Cumberland Gap into the rich and pristine Kentucky wilderness.

Born in 1875, Dr. Laswell went to college, became a teacher, and eventually graduated from medical school in Louisville, Kentucky. David learned from his research that much has been written about his grandfather, Dr. Laswell, as being a respected physician, farmer and businessman before dying of cancer in 1945.[xxii]

In 1899, William D. Laswell married a young woman whose first and middle names would be spelled in various ways in times to come. On her gravestone, her name is rendered Letia Cumile Laswell. Together, they brought six children into the world, of whom George would be the last.

Less than two months after giving birth to George, Letia contracted a terrible infection called erysipelas. At a later time, it would be curable with antibiotics, but in 1913, these wonder drugs had not been invented or discovered.

The infection may have started as a scratch or abrasion, and it could have spread from bacteria in her nasal passages. Within two days, she may have been afflicted with a high fever, shaking, chills, skin lesions or pox.

It happened while she was visiting her family. Six days after the infection appeared, she breathed her last—leaving this world at 3 o'clock on a September morning. She had been under a doctor's care for several days.

George's mother was 31 years old, and he was about 10 weeks old when he lost her.

The obituary in the September 5, 1913, Mount Vernon (Kentucky) Signal said: "It came as a great shock to her host of friends and relatives, when the word was given out on Tuesday afternoon that there was no possible chance for her recovery and that the final summons was only a matter of a few hours." The newspaper said Letia "was one of those saintly characters that to know her was an inspiration and blessing."

Shortly afterwards, Dr. Laswell married Eunice, who became George's stepmother. Together, they had six children.

On October 15, 1928, Eunice died of eclampsia while delivering twins, a boy and a girl. She was 43 years old. At the age of 15, George Laswell lost his second mother. A few weeks later, Celia, one of the newborn twins, died.

The events are tragically reminiscent of Hortense Huffman's own birth, when her mother and twin sister died and were lost to the world.

In 1929, Dr. Laswell married Lucille, with whom he had three children.

In making these discoveries, David Workman finally answered two of the questions he had wondered about—where he and Cynthia got their first names.

"David," it turns out, is a name that was handed down for several generations in the Laswell family. Dr. William David Laswell was undoubtedly named for his own father, David. In turn, Dr. and Letia Cumile Laswell passed the name to George's older brother, William David Jr.—known to many as simply David. When George and Hortense named their own son David, he became the fourth consecutive generation to acquire the name. In 2008, David Workman's grandson, John David, became the fifth generation to carry on the name, after he was born to daughter Kirsten Cynthia and son-in-law Paul Feenan.

In Rockcastle County, Kentucky, there are other Laswells carrying on the name of David in the 21st Century. And some carry the name "Lee." They, like David Workman, are descendants of David and Flurry or Flury or Flora Jane Laswell.

"Cynthia" was the name of a younger sister of George Laswell. Cynthia Workman's unknown aunt lived a full life, but never knew the marvelous human being who carried her name, or the wonderful young women who continue to carry it on in the Workman family.

George's home life must have been challenging. For many years, he was one of the older children in the home, but not the oldest. In all, he had 14 siblings, two of whom died very young.

He apparently graduated from high school in Kings Mountain, Kentucky, then attended nearby Berea College for a year. In April 1942, with World War II in full swing, George was inducted into the U.S. Army in Cincinnati, Ohio, at the age of 28.

Just shy of 19 months later, with a lot of the war yet to be fought and won, Private First Class George Laswell was honorably discharged from the Army.

Ironically, he spent his Army time at Fort Lewis, located between Tacoma and Olympia, Washington.

Four decades later, the former son who never knew him would move his own family to the outskirts of Olympia, to within a skip and a hop of that same military base. George's granddaughters—unknown to him—would grow up there, graduate from high school there, and graduate from a university within virtual walking distance of Fort Lewis.

George's discharge certification does not give a specific reason for his early release from military service, but it lists his character as "Excellent." Early honorable discharges were far from the norm during a world war in which the vast majority of enlistees and draftees were inducted "for the duration."

George's service record would entitle him to burial in the Golden Gate National Cemetery in San Bruno after a fatal heart attack on February 1966 in Fresno, California. After his Army discharge, George apparently returned to Kentucky around the end of 1943 or beginning of 1944.

In July 1945, George was listed as the person who reported his father's death in Lexington, Kentucky, after a protracted battle with cancer. Sometime after Dr. Laswell's death, his widow Lucille moved north to Dayton, Ohio, with their youngest daughter. They would make Ohio their home.

Upon learning this, David Workman would wonder whether it was family connection that led George to Dayton in the late 1940s. This will likely remain one of the many unknowns and unknowables about his birth father.

David eventually obtained a copy of George's death certificate in Fresno, California. It would answer some long-unanswered questions.

Five years after writing his 1961 letter to Gene Workman in Loudonville, Ohio, George was working in Fresno as a self-employed nurseryman and had a wife, Lillian, in Sacramento.

Two weeks after arriving in Fresno, George was pronounced dead at Fresno County Hospital, and an autopsy determined that he had been killed by a coronary thrombosis brought on by coronary sclerosis and generalized arteriosclerosis. The autopsy revealed that his heart attack wasn't his first. Years before, he had suffered one.

It occurred to David that it was possible George was not exaggerating when he called Luella Smith on the phone in early 1952, telling her he had almost died.

Whatever happened to him after he left David in Alabama, George came to regret his actions, as he demonstrated in his 1961 letter to his former stepson, Gene.

One of the ironies of George's life and death was the fact that, at his death, the embalmer's name was Loudon, the same name as the founder of the town where he had lived so briefly with Hortense, their children and his stepsons.

As an adult—husband, father, grandfather—David Workman would take note of words in a favorite country song, about a boy who didn't know his father and didn't want to know why. Now, at last, he was free to wonder why. Why he never knew George, his birth father. Why Cynthia never knew her birth father.

What made George do the things he did, and not do the things a father does?

Why did George decide to take David on that journey that led to Alabama? And why did he then leave him? Why did he leave Cynthia behind?

What caused George Laswell to drift about? What winds blew him to the places he lit a while, including Mobile and San Diego and Fresno, before he reached his final resting place at the Golden Gate National Cemetery?

David would come to believe that George's gift to him, besides birth, was staying out of the picture—not meddling in the lives of the children he abandoned so long ago.

One day, David and Clover will visit the site of George's grave in the Golden Gate National Cemetery. There among thousands of heroes, they will stand in front of a white headstone engraved with a cross and bearing this inscription:

George Shelton Laswell
Kentucky
PFC Co. C
778 MP BN
World War II
June 20, 1913
February 1, 1966

And there, in George's presence, David Workman will say aloud what he has said before: "I forgive you, George. I believe Cynthia has forgiven you. We didn't have to walk in your shoes, and for that we are thankful. God bless you."

−30−[xxiii]

Passages

David came to understand that an essential part of living, and growing, is saying goodbye. Over the sixty-plus years since his brother Ralph and sister-in-law Louise became his dad and his mom, there have been many goodbyes, none of them easy.

Grandparents Jessie and Charles Alley

In his early childhood, David gained Charles Ephraim Alley and Jessie Gilson Alley as his grandparents in Nashville, Tennessee. In the home they built on Murphy Road, they reared their son Clarence, daughters Katie and Charlsie and Louise. Louise's children, Danny and Peggy, loved them, and their house. It was a safe place for the children after their own father died in a work place accident at the beginning of World War II.

Charles and Jessie lived long lives and left a big imprint on their grandchildren, including Dan and Peggy and eventually David. During some difficult times in Louise's life, "Granddaddy" and Grandma Alley reared Danny. Their front yard became the scene of one of David's earliest memories when Ralph brought David here on their trip back to Ohio from Mobile, Alabama.

Charles and his business partner, M.H. Parrotte, operated a successful construction contracting firm called Alley & Parrotte, for many years. Grandpa Alley's specialty was building impressive, durable stone bridges, dams and houses.

Grandpa and Grandma Alley each had a foot in two different worlds. He was born February 26, 1879; she on March 28, 1881. They were part of the first generation born after America's devastating Civil War and the assassination of President Lincoln. They lived through World Wars I and II into the Cold War, when mechanized killing took place on a massive scale unheard of in the previous history of humankind.

Grandma died January 10, 1955, at age 73, and Grandpa followed on April 4, 1957, at age 78. Losing them was very hard for Louise, Dan and Peggy. Before Grandma Alley died in a Nashville hospital room, she asked for her beloved Danny, and

Louise and Ralph immediately got both Danny and Peggy onto a commercial flight to Nashville—a rarity in the '50s. Boeing hadn't yet launched the world's first commercial jet; they flew on a plane powered by propellers. When the teenagers arrived in Jessie's hospital room, they were notified that Grandma was in a coma and wouldn't know they were there. Danny picked up her hand, and Grandma looked at him and said, "I knew you would come." She closed her eyes and was gone.

Grandma Alley lives on through the cooking that Dan and Peggy learned at her side. One specialty, which Dan has mastered, is Grandma's scrambled eggs. Nobody scrambles eggs like the ones that Dan cooks just as Grandma taught him.

Rhea Stouffer

Rhea, born in 1899, was six or seven years older than David's mother Hortense. She became an integral member of the Workman and Laswell family. From all accounts, Hortense couldn't have provided for her family in difficult times without Rhea's help as the housekeeper and nanny for her boys. Then, after Hortense's death, Rhea became the stand-in mom as well as housekeeper for the family that Gene held together with little to no help from his stepfather, George.

After rearing Cynthia for some five years, Rhea had to give her up when the courts granted adoption to Cynthia's and David's brother Gene and sister-in-law Mickey Workman. Rhea continued to be an important person in Cynthia's and David's lives—especially Cynthia's. In 1962, she passed away and was buried in the Loudonville Cemetery at age 63. Cynthia remained loyal to Rhea's family; one of the people whom Cynthia and new husband John visited on their wedding day was Rhea's sister, Bessie, in Loudonville. To Cynthia, she would always be Aunt Bessie.

Luella Smith

Luella "Nanny" Smith died in 1963 at 65 years of age. Her life stretched back to the previous century and a different world, 1897. Born near the end of the horse and buggy era, she never drove a car, and regularly rode the bus.

In the 1920s, she married Carl Smith Sr., who had come from Virginia to work as a ship fitter at Mobile. The two of them bought three or four rural acres on Greenleaf Road, cleared the property for a garden, chickens, and pasturage for a horse. Carl could build most anything with his hands, and it's likely he built the modest clapboard home where children were reared and where David Laswell Workman spent six months in Luella's care.

She was a founding member of the Cottage Hill Baptist Church and a valued member of the congregation. In 1963, Luella was buried with husband Carl at Pinecrest Cemetery, a few miles from her home.

Grandmother Marie Workman

Marie Workman, second wife of Ralph Workman Sr., was 66 years old when she died in 1970 after a long illness.

David and his family knew next to nothing about her life before her marriage to Ralph Sr., but there is a picture of her as a 16-year-old, and she seems almost glamorous.

Marie and Ralph met in Cleveland, and then he divorced Hortense, with whom he had three sons. Marie and Ralph were married in 1942 and moved to Loudonville about 1946, the year Ralph's mother Viola passed away.

There is no doubt Marie adored Ralph and he adored her. Moving from the big city to a small town where everybody knows everybody's business, and where divorce was unheard of in the 1940s, was unquestionably an act of love on Marie's part.

Ralph and Marie had great years together. They spent many winters in Florida, away from the cold, snowy climate of northern Ohio. Photos show them dressed in tropical style, including swimsuits. They look like they could be movie stars of the era. For grandchildren looking at the pictures, it's hard to make these lovebirds be the "Grandpa" and "Grandma" of their memories.

David's Grandma Workman got along famously with Louise, the wife of Ralph Jr. When they were together a couple of times each year, these two outgoing women had a great time together. There was a lot of laughter.

David's last memory of Marie came shortly before her death. He and his new bride made the 110-mile drive from Springfield to Mansfield to visit her in the hospital. However, his 21-year-old brain and sentimentality would not allow him to accept the reality—the finality—of his grandmother's situation. In his happy-talk state of mind, he wasn't a comfort to his grieving grandfather. This did not diminish in any way his love for them, or the lasting memory of Granddad Workman with tears in his eyes.

Sister Cynthia Workman Rohr

From 1950 to 1971, Cynthia made a larger-than-life impact on the people who loved her, and on the next generations after her.

She never knew the warmth of her mother's arms, but two women would take her into their arms. Rhea Stouffer reared her from 1951 to 1956. In that year, Mickey Workman became her mother for the rest of her life.

Cynthia didn't know her birth father, George Laswell, but her brother Gene Workman became her father and was everything that a father can be.

In 1971, at the too-young age of 21, she died of complications from kidney disease, and husband John Rohr became a widower in his early 20s.

Cynthia's funeral was held in St. Joseph Catholic Church in Canton, Ohio, with all of her Ohio family, and John's, gathered around. Her Laswell family from Kentucky never knew her.

One of her brother David's lasting memories of the funeral Mass would be the young altar boy, who was wearing sneakers beneath his altar robe. In those days when funerals were much more formal than they would be during his lifetime, the young boy in the sneakers made an impact on David, adding a down-to-earth touch to an elaborate funeral service. "Cynthia would like that," David told himself.

David regretted that he did not have the opportunity to give to her one of his kidneys, in hopes of extending the life of the sister whom he loved, admired, and would forever after miss deeply.

She was buried in Calvary Cemetery in Canton. Her grave is so far from those who loved, and love, her. Thanks be to God for heaven, for she is most certainly there. And there, she is not alone.

On this earth, her legacy continues in the hearts and memories of all who knew her, and in the ensuing generations of beautiful women who carry her name.

Aunt Grace Koppert

This wonderful woman lived on this earth from 1885 to 1972. She never gave birth to a child with her own DNA, but was a mother to four of them—two by adoption, one through foster care, and one because Fred Huffman called upon her.

In 1906, she became the surrogate mother for Hortense, the daughter of cousins Fred and Della Huffman, upon Della's tragic death. After Grace married Bill Koppert, she became the stepmother to his daughter and son. The daughter died in a traffic accident while she was a college student. Grace also took in a foster daughter.

It was during a visit with Grace that Hortense suffered a heart attack and then died in childbirth in 1950.

From Bill's death in 1955, Grace lived alone until her death in 1972 at age 86. She is buried at North Liberty Cemetery a few miles west of Jelloway, Ohio.

Louise Workman, David's mom

David's and Dan's and Peggy's mom left this earth in 1981 when nobody was ready to give her up. Earlier in the year, she had undergone a desperate surgery in hopes that her cancer could be removed from her body.

Immediately after the operation, the surgeon delivered the dreadful news to Ralph Jr., Dan, Peggy and David. Her remaining months would not be quality time, as most people would define it.

The death of a parent can break a family apart, or it can bring a family closer. In Louise's case, it drew David and Dan and Peggy even closer than they had previously been. And they had always been close.

The days and nights spent together in the hospital before and after the unsuccessful surgery made the three children of Louise Workman appreciate each other even more than before, and their bond of love grew ever stronger.

One highlight of Louise's final months was an event that she looked eagerly forward to—the marriage of grandson Steve to granddaughter-to-be Jodi, due to occur in the fall. In David's long-distance conversations with his mom during the intervening months, she was interested in two subjects— whether David and family would be moving back to Ohio and the excitement about Steve's and Jodi's wedding.

In the first half of 1981, David had looked all over for a newspaper job within a day's drive or so of Springfield. From the kitchen table in the house just outside Marysville, Washington, across the Snohomish River from Everett, David sent letter after letter to potential newspaper employers. He had interviews in Cleveland, Ohio, and Buffalo, New York, but he didn't land either job. Finally, he did land one, and just in time before his severance pay from the Everett Herald ran out. His new employer was the morning newspaper in Spokane, Washington. His job—and his family's home—would be located in Olympia, the state capital, 90 miles south of Everett.

David hated to tell his mom the news that he would not be moving closer to home. "I wish you could be nearer," she said on the phone that night.

As Steve's and Jodi's wedding approached, each detail pleased Louise. She so wished she could be there, but knew she was too weak, too fragile. Soon after the wedding, Louise finally allowed death to take her away, at age 60. There was no doubt in David's mind that she held on for them.

In the months before Peggy lost her one and only mother, a friend of hers and husband Dan Quinn made available side-by-side cemetery plots in a beautiful spot called Rose Hill Burial Park on South Charleston Pike, a few miles east of Springfield's city limits.

For David, this final resting place made it somehow easier to say goodbye to the woman who had invested her love and care and wisdom, and many sacrifices, into making him the man he became.

David was given the privilege of suggesting the words that would grace Louise's gravesite. With the agreement of Dan and Peggy and their dad, the grave marker would say to the world: "She made a difference."

Most certainly, she made all the difference.

Grandfather Ralph Workman Sr.

Ralph O. Workman Sr. died in 1986 at the age of 83, in Springfield. He had lived the last several years of his life with his oldest son, Ralph Jr., at the house on Beacon Street. He was living there in 1981 when daughter-in-law Louise died of cancer.

In Springfield, he was close to his son Jack and family, as well as Ralph's daughter Peggy's family. The neighbor children adopted Ralph Sr. as their grandfather, and on any summer night they were likely to come next door to be with him on the front porch of the two-story charcoal-gray, asbestos-shingled house.

Ralph Sr.'s best friend in those years was Spotty, the little black and white terrier that became a big part of the personality of the house on Beacon Street. The elder gentleman and the little terrier spent hours together at Ralph Sr.'s stuffed rocking chair in the front room.

In the summer of 1984, when David and family were visiting Springfield from Olympia, Washington, Ralph Sr. allowed the grandson to record an oral history of life as he had known it. Years later, David transcribed it, and it remains a treasured gift, worth more than gold.

In one of the most important interviews of his life, David the journalist learned the history of the Workman / Stacher farm at the hill on East Main Street at the edge of Loudonville. He also first learned the story of the Workmans leaving the Netherlands to travel to the New World in 1647, and how later generations migrated to the Maryland-Pennsylvania border country, where they eventually sold their farms to a coal mining company in the early 1800s. The money from the sale of the farms allowed several Workman families to migrate westward, some going into the region that became West Virginia while others went northwest into Ohio. Ralph described his own branch of the Workmans settling first near Jelloway and later just outside Loudonville.

Ralph also recalled his youth in and around Loudonville. As a school boy, he worked at his father's grocery store in the mornings and after school. Before World War I, he owned one of the first radios in Loudonville, and remembered that it got exactly one station, KDKA in Pittsburgh, which carried exactly one kind of programming—weather reports.

As a teen, he roamed the hills and forests and streams several miles around Loudonville, trapping muskrats and raccoons and foxes. And with his dog, he hunted quail and rabbits and would roast them over a fire and eat them with beans and bread. He recalled shooting copperhead snakes, a venomous pit viper, but never seeing rattlers. He usually hunted and camped alone.

Under David's questioning, his grandfather recalled some of the interesting older people he had known in childhood—a woman who was said to be a niece of Jonathan Chapman, also known as Johnny Appleseed; another woman who, as a young girl, had traveled with her family in wagon train from Florida to Oregon; and old Tommy Wilson, a plasterer by trade, who would tell him stories of the Civil War, including the Union and Confederate soldiers in trenches so close to one another that they would "throw tobacco back and forth."

Of all the stories that Ralph Sr. told his grandson, none animated the elderly grandfather quite so much as his stories of trips with Marie from Florida to Havana, Cuba, before the fall of Batista to Fidel Castro's revolutionaries.

He loved the vibe and the colonial architecture of Cuban capital city on the Caribbean Sea. In his eighties, Ralph Sr. no longer traveled, not even from Springfield to Loudonville. However, he would go in a heartbeat, he said, if he could return just one more time to Havana.

Three decades later, David would smile at the thought that his grandfather, a lifelong Republican, would be celebrating when the then Democratic U.S. President decided it was time for the United States to end its ban on travel and trade with Cuba.

In the summer of 1986, Ralph Sr.'s funeral was held at the Methodist Church in Loudonville, where his mother and his grandparents had worshiped. His body joined Marie's at the top of a hill in Loudonville's cemetery. There, they are surrounded by numerous Workman, Priest and Stacher ancestors. Not far away are the gravesites of Hortense Workman Laswell, buried among her Huffman family.

Ralph Workman Jr., David's dad

After the death of Louise in 1981, Ralph Jr. swore that he would never marry again. He never did. No one, he said, could replace the beautiful, outgoing woman from Nashville with whom he had spent thirty of his happiest years.

Together, they had spent many years as bowling partners. Both were quite good, and Ralph would frequently hit the 200's. Together, after the children were gone, they had hit the road together going cross-country on sightseeing trips. In 1980, they visited David's family in Everett, Washington, enjoying precious time with granddaughters Kara and Kirsten and letting David drive them on a loop trip through the dramatic Cascade Mountains.

Around 1986, Ralph retired from trucking and drew his pension from the Teamsters Union and Social Security. After the death of Ralph Sr. and of Spotty, the house on Beacon Street became very lonely and Ralph sold it, moving to the perfect apartment downtown in the former, glorious Shawnee Hotel, which had been transformed into apartments for senior citizens. From his unit, he had a sweeping view over the city to the northern reaches of Springfield. It was the ideal place to spend his summers. Winters, he spent in Myrtle Beach, a little resort town on the coast of South Carolina.

At the Workman home in Washington State, Saturday mornings were special because the phone would ring and David's dad would be on the other end. They would chat for a few minutes about anything at all. And then they would pick up the conversation again on the following Saturday. On Nov. 30, 1996, they had their last conversation. The next day, David's and Dan's and Peggy's father collapsed on his bed at the Shawnee Apartments, while packing for the trip south to Myrtle Beach. Peggy, the faithful daughter, found his body on Monday morning.

In the last 15 years of his life, Ralph had at least two lady friends, but he never again married. After his death, his children found an envelope in the glove box of their father's car. In it were photos of Ralph's and Louise's final road trip together in 1980.

At age 70, Ralph O. Workman Jr. was buried next to Louise at Rose Hill Burial Park, just outside Springfield, Ohio, along the road to South Charleston, under the filtered light of carefully placed shade trees.

When son David wrote a tribute to his father and sent it to the Springfield News–Sun, columnist Tom Stafford interviewed David, Dan and Peggy, and wrote a wonderful column that the family would treasure forever. The article was a testimony to the heart, soul and character of a good man, who took in and reared three children, none of whom were his responsibility until he made them so.

An unexpected thing about the death of one's parents is finding gifts and mementoes that you have given them. In 1996, one of the things that came back into David's hands was a copy of a book he had authored, published in 1988 by the Tacoma News Tribune, under the title: "Washington: A Centennial Portrait."

Inside the front cover, David had written: "To Dad—I owe you everything. With deepest love,

Your son, David"

Truer words were never written or spoken.

Brother Gene Workman

Of Hortense Workman Laswell's five children, the one who made the biggest impact on his communities and on the betterment of a great many children was Gene.

He was also deeply loyal to his brothers. With wife Mickey, he made it a point to stay in close touch with David and David's family throughout their lives. They made many trips to the Pacific Northwest to visit their Washington State family. They also helped their children and several grandchildren make the trip to the Pacific Northwest.

In August 2000, Gene brought son-in-law Brian, grandson Kent and grandson Nicholas to Vancouver, British Columbia, Canada, where David and son-in-law Tim picked them up at the airport and took them to Whistler in Canada's rugged coastal mountain range.

A few months after the trip to Canada, Gene was diagnosed with an advanced case of mesothelioma, the cancer that is caused by asbestos fibers burying themselves in the cells around the lungs.

In Gene's case, the culprit had been the engine room of the USS Helena, on which Gene had served as a Machinist's Mate from 1951 to 1955.

Gene was a patriotic American through and through, and he believed in service to one's country and community and to God. He refused to complain about the Navy's decision to knowingly expose him and many thousands more sailors to deadly asbestos in the form of fire retardant in ships throughout the fleet.

After receiving the diagnosis, Gene bought an airline ticket so his younger brother could come visit him in the summer of 2001. They had a wonderful week together and, as always, made the drive together from near Orrville, Ohio, to Loudonville.

Another benefit of that Ohio trip was that it allowed David to spend a couple of days with sister Peggy in Springfield. She was in the late stages of throat cancer. This would be David's last visit with a brother and a sister who meant so much to him. Gene died in December 2001—almost exactly five years after older brother Ralph Sr.

In the course of his life, Gene served as president of Massillon's home town bank and then president and chairman of Orville's home town bank.

He was active in supporting the Boy Scouts of America—ever mindful that Scouting had made all the difference for him during his years as a stranger in a strange city, Dayton. When brother David informed him in late 1991 that he had agreed to serve as Scoutmaster of Boy Scout Troop 266 at the Lutheran Church of the Good Shepherd in Olympia, Gene said: "God bless you, Dave. Kids need Scouting. I know it saved me."

Gene was active in his churches in Loudonville, Massillon and Orville, and in the Boys and Girls Clubs, which are dedicated to helping young people achieve their full potential.

Gene's life is still making a difference in the lives of children and families. At his retirement, his bank board of directors gave a substantial gift to an endowment fund of the Boys and Girls Clubs in Orrville, home of Smucker's jellies and jams. It is the Eugene Workman Scholarship Fund.

And after Gene's death, wife Mickey and children Mark, Carol, Cathy and Cheryl made the family decision to seek a financial settlement for their father's asbestos-induced death—from a large class-action claim that made billions of dollars available from the industry that produced asbestos.

The family used the money from the settlement to establish a scholarship fund; and each year, a scholarship is awarded in memory of the Workman family.

Gene was laid to rest at age 68 in the Loudonville Cemetery on a hillside not far from Hortense and Huffman family members, and not far from his father and many Workman and Stacher ancestors. His light still shines brightly.

Sister Peggy Quinn

Peggy Welch was in seventh grade when her mother, Louise, announced that she and Ralph Workman Jr. would be married and that Peggy and brother Dan would be moving from Grandma and Grandpa Alley's home in Nashville, Tennessee, to Springfield, Ohio.

In 1996, in a newspaper tribute to Ralph Jr., Peggy recalled for columnist Tom Stafford that her first question for her mother was "why did she have to marry somebody and take me from Nashville?"[xxiv]

Soon after Peggy and Dan arrived at the little house on Beatrice Street in Springfield, they learned that their new stepfather's little brother had vanished with his own father.

It would have been so easy and so understandable for Peggy and Dan to resent this news and wonder what kind of family they were getting into. However, they wholeheartedly joined in Ralph's and Louise's decision to find little David and bring him home where he belonged.

From the very first time that Davy came into the family, his new teenage sister and brother treated him exactly as if he had been born into their family. There are photos of Davy with Peggy, and of Davy standing under an arch of human arms created by Dan and one of his buddies.

As years passed, and Peggy married school sweetheart Dan Quinn, David would spend many nights and weekends at their house. Their children would become practically his little brothers and sister.

At age 29, Peggy was diagnosed with a rare cancer in her sinus cavity. A doctor told the family she might live six months. However, there was a new form of treatment that might be worth trying. It was called "cobalt." It was a forerunner of radiation treatment.

While the young mother underwent those awful treatments, the rest of the family pitched in to help with the children. David's job was ironing clothes—an unavoidable necessity in the era before wrinkle-free, wash-and-wear fabrics were available. David became pretty handy with spray starch and an iron, and the ironing skills served him for the rest of his working years.

Peggy and the cobalt treatments beat the odds, although the radiation permanently destroyed tissues in her neck and mouth. She lived another thirty years before another aggressive cancer attacked her. She would know her grandchildren, and they would know her.

After moving to Springfield with her mother and brother Dan in 1951, Peggy quickly came to accept and then to love the big man who was her new father. In the last years of Ralph's life as a widower, she took care of his bill paying and other responsibilities so he could spend winters in South Carolina. She was a devoted daughter.

Cancer finally claimed her life in May 2002 at age 62 on the day when David's twin granddaughters, Peggy's grandnieces, were born a continent away. She is buried at Rose Hill Burial Park, not far from Louise and Ralph Jr., the parents who loved her, and whom she loved.

Brother Jack Workman

Jack Workman was born in 1936 in Loudonville, and spent his earliest years surrounded by parents, grandmother, two older brothers, lots of cousins and great-aunts and great-uncles, and a town full of people who knew the Workmans and Huffmans.

At age six, after his parents' divorce, Jack and older brother Gene moved with their mother, Hortense, to Dayton where she worked at Frigidaire at Wright Field Army Air Corps installation through World War II into the late 1940s.

In 1942, Jack gained a stepmother when Ralph Workman Sr. married Marie.

After Jack's mother Hortense remarried, gave birth to two more children, moved the family back to Loudonville, and died very suddenly in 1950, Jack's world was undoubtedly turned upside down.

His older brother, Gene, became a surrogate father to Jack and one-year-old David and newborn Cynthia. When Gene left for service in the Navy in 1951, Jack moved in with Ralph Workman Sr. and stepmother Marie. Like brother Gene before him, Jack joined the Navy. He served in the submarine service after high school in the late 1950s.

In the early 1960s, he moved to Springfield to be near his oldest brother, Junior, and family. For a time, he lived with Junior, Louise and David until finding a job and getting settled. He remained in Springfield until his death in 2006, marrying wife Margaret and rearing sons Jack Jr. and Peter. Early in their marriage, Jack and Margaret lived within walking distance of his brothers and Louise, and David visited them frequently. In Springfield, Jack would be known as a hard worker, delivering soda pop by the case to locations all around the area until retiring.

For most of his life, Jack had a close relationship with his brothers and sister. In 1974 or 1975, the "Workman boys"— Ralph Sr., Ralph Jr., Gene, Jack, David and Gene's son, Mark— went on a road trip together to a Cincinnati Reds home game. On this occasion, Jack gave David an old, grainy snapshot, and said: "This is a picture of your dad." At the time, David was perplexed because his dad was Ralph Jr., the brother who had been his true father. It would be many years, decades really, before David would appreciate the photo—the only known picture of George Laswell and David and Cynthia (both of them barely toddlers).

After Ralph Workman Sr.'s death in 1986, things changed. Jack withdrew from his brothers and their families. When Jack died in November 2006 at age 70, David learned about his death when brother-in-law Dan Quinn read the notice in the Springfield newspaper.

Whatever had come between the brothers, younger brother David could not bring himself to assign blame. Jack had a very challenging childhood. David would choose to remember Jack as a brother he loved, a brother who had loved him.

Jack is buried in the Dayton National Cemetery by virtue of his honorable service in the United States Navy.

Hortense Huffman / Workman / Laswell

During her short lifetime between 1906 and 1950, Hortense had no opportunity and no reason to visit the State of Washington in the far northwestern corner of the 48 states that then existed. Her life took place in and around Loudonville and Dayton, Ohio, with family trips to Michigan and Florida. However, there is a place in Olympia, Washington, where she is memorialized.

In 1999, David Workman's family in Olympia had the opportunity to purchase a plaque for her. It is inlaid into the walkway surrounding the Evergreen State's World War II Memorial on the Capitol Campus. The plaque is inscribed: "Hortense Huffman / Defense Worker / Love, Your Family." Someone reading the inscription needs only glance up to see the magnificent domed and columned State Capitol a short walk away. It is appropriate for Hortense to be remembered for the work she did to keep armaments and equipment flowing to the Allied Forces that won the greatest war in history. It is also appropriate because three generations of her family have made Washington State their home.

After Hortense's memorial was in place, David realized that, for the first time, he and his own family had been able to do something of lasting value for the mother whom he had lost only 13 months into his life, the woman of whom he had no personal memory. He was deeply thankful.

. . .

And then there remained. . .

Among all of David's generation in his known family, and of all the preceding generations, there now remain these four members:

184 |

David Workman lives a life, in gratitude, in Olympia, Washington, with a wife who loves him, and with daughters and stepdaughters, sons-in-law, and grandchildren in two states.

Dan Welch, who was known all through his Springfield school years as Danny Workman, and Dan's wife Judy, live near Nashville, Tennessee. Their three sons and daughters-in-law and many grandchildren live in many states.

Brother-in-law Dan Quinn lives in Springfield with wife, Ramona, whom he met in church and married after Peggy's death. Dan's two sons and daughter, and many grandchildren, live in several states.

Mickey Workman, Gene's steadfast wife and companion and partner in life, lives at Dalton, Ohio, between Wooster and Massillon. Their four children and their spouses and many grandchildren live in many parts of the United States.

These four, the last of their generation of the Workman family, hold each other dear. They stay close, across the miles. They are the family that Louise, Ralph Jr. and Hortense would surely want them to be.

Dan and Peg, the outgoing red-heads of the family

David with his brothers-turned-fathers
—Ralph and Gene—in the 1990s

Ralph, Louise and their kids—Dan, Peggy and David
in their '70s look

Mickey, Gene, Cynthia, Mark, Carol (left, standing),
Cathy (right) and little Cheryl

Gene and Mickey and family, fund-raising against diabetes, 2001

Timeline of Events
in *Letter from Alabama*

1647

Dirck Jans Woertman / Wortman / Workman boards a sailing ship in the Netherlands, and migrates to New Amsterdam, settling in the Dutch colonial settlement of Brooklyn, where he later marries Marretje Denyse.

1664

William Lasswell migrates from England to colonial West New Jersey. Some of his descendants will settle the Kentucky frontier.

1732

Melchior Stacher / Stecher / Stecker migrates from the Palatinate, western Germany, to the British colony of Pennsylvania. His family will eventually thrive and multiply in the rural part of Pennsylvania south of Pittsburgh. A branch of the family tree will transplant itself in Ohio. David Stacher will become a prominent businessman in Loudonville and build the farm buildings that become a central part of the lives of his Workman descendants for decades to come.

1770s

In 1775, frontiersman Daniel Boone blazes a trail from Cumberland Gap in the Appalachian Mountains into Kentucky to lead settlers into a region that, until now has been a rich and bountiful hunting ground for Native American tribes. Over time, this trace becomes the Wilderness Road, which brings hundreds of thousands of settlers.

Joseph Clark is born in, or possibly brought to, the frontier region of Kentucky, which becomes a part of Virginia before gaining statehood in 1792. He marries Judith, also called Julia. One of their descendants will be George S. Laswell, who will grow up in Kings Mountain, Kentucky.

1780-1800

Laswells and Abneys migrate to the Kentucky frontier in the region that will become Rockcastle, Madison, Estill and Lincoln counties.

1814

James Loudon Priest purchases 160 acres of north-central Ohio frontier and begins platting Loudonville. His granddaughter, Jerutia, will marry Morgan Workman.

1828

Christian and Magdalena Spreng / Sprang leave the village of Schweighausen in Alsace, France, and migrate to America, settling in Holmes County, Ohio. One of their descendants will be Della Spreng, who marries Fred Huffman and gives birth to Hortense.

1832

After Henry Hoffman / Huffman Sr. and wife Eva leave the village of Lembach in Alsace for the long trip across the Atlantic, they eventually settle in Holmes County, Ohio.

Martin and Barbara Heffelfinger arrive in Holmes County, having left their home village of Hoffen in Alsace. One of their grandchildren will be Fred Huffman.

1840s

Morgan and Jerutia Priest Workman build a cabin of hewn logs. In this small and modest home, they will rear a large family. In 1963, the cabin will be moved to Loudonville's Central Park as a lasting tribute to the early settlers of the community.

1898

Della Spreng and Fred Huffman are married in Loudonville, Ohio.

1899

William David Laswell and Letia Cumile Reams are married in Rockcastle County, Kentucky.

1903

Ralph O. Workman is born in Loudonville, Ohio, to Harry and Viola Workman.

1906

Hortense Huffman is born to Fred and Della Huffman. Her twin sister dies in childbirth. Within a few days, Della dies.

Grace Berry Koppert, a cousin, is called upon to serve as nanny and surrogate mother to Hortense throughout her childhood.

1913

George S. Laswell is born in Mount Vernon, Kentucky, to Dr. William David and Letia Cumile Laswell. He will grow up in tiny Kings Mountain, Kentucky, one of 15 siblings.

Ten weeks after his birth, George's mother dies.

Dr. Laswell marries Eunice Parker Ball, who becomes George's new mother.

1924

Hortense Huffman graduates from Loudonville High School.

Shortly afterward, 18-year-old Hortense and 21-year-old Ralph Workman are married in Loudonville.

1926

Ralph O. Workman Jr. is born to Ralph and Hortense Workman

1928

Eunice Parker Laswell, second wife of Dr. Laswell and stepmother of George S. Laswell, dies in childbirth.

1929

Dr. Laswell marries Lucille Young; George and siblings gain a new mother. They give birth to three children.

1933

Gene Workman is born to Ralph and Hortense Workman

1936

Jack Workman is born to Ralph and Hortense Workman

1941

About this time, Ralph Workman Sr. divorces Hortense.

Japan attacks the United States Navy fleet in Pearl Harbor, Hawaii, setting in motion America's declaration of war against Japan, Nazi Germany and Fascist Italy.

Hortense commutes to and from Wooster Business College, Ohio, eventually earning a diploma to operate International Business Machines (IBM) punch card equipment.

1942

Ralph Workman Sr. marries Marie.

About this time, teenager Ralph Workman Jr. leaves home and strikes out on his own in Cleveland, Ohio.

Hortense lands a job at Frigidaire, a division of General Motors, in Dayton, Ohio, to participate in the company's conversion to War Production, helping to supply the Allied military forces in World War II.

George Laswell from Kings Mountain, Kentucky, is inducted into the United States Army at Cincinnati, Ohio.

1943

Hortense and sons Gene and Jack are among the first occupants of the barracks-style apartments in Overlook Homes, one of several government projects that provide housing to families of workers in the War Production industries in the area. Rhea Stouffer joins the family as a housekeeper and child-care provider.

Some 18 months after his induction, Private First Class George Laswell receives an honorable discharge from the Army at Fort Lewis, between Tacoma and Olympia, Washington.

1945

World War II ends in victory by the United States and Allied forces.

Dr. Laswell dies at a hospital in Lexington, Kentucky.

In Mobile, Alabama, Carl G. Smith Sr. suffers a fatal heart attack, leaving a widow, Luella, and five children.

Luella earns income for her family as a nanny / child-care provider.

1946

Viola Stacher Workman, mother of Ralph O. Workman Sr., dies in Loudonville. She leaves several properties to her only surviving son. She leaves her family's farm on East Main Street, at the east edge of Loudonville, to her three grandsons: Ralph Jr., Gene and Jack.

Ralph Workman Sr. moves back to Loudonville with wife Marie.

1947

Ralph Workman Jr. is living in Springfield, Ohio, driving for Fugate and Girton Driveway (trucking) Company.

1948

George Laswell and Hortense Workman, who meet in Dayton, are married.

1949

David Lee Laswell is born in Dayton to George and Hortense Laswell.

Hortense and George move from Dayton to Loudonville with Gene, Jack and newborn David.

Hortense and George learn that they will be having a second child—Hortense's fifth.

The Cox newspaper company establishes the Journal Herald, a new morning newspaper in Dayton—combining the Journal and the Herald, which were acquired the previous year.

1950

During a visit to Mount Vernon, Ohio, Hortense Laswell suffers a heart attack; delivers her first and only daughter, Cynthia; and then dies of a second heart attack the next morning.

The Korean War begins. The first U.S. ground troops are deployed in that Asian nation.

After Hortense's death, housekeeper and child-care provider Rhea Stouffer becomes a mainstay in the care of infants David and Cynthia Laswell in Loudonville.

1951

Gene Workman graduates from Loudonville High School and registers, as required, for the military draft.

He enlists in the Navy and is stationed in California as a crew member of the cruiser USS Helena.

14-year-old Jack Workman moves in with his father, Ralph Workman Sr., and stepmother, Marie.

George Laswell leaves Loudonville, taking two-year-old David and one-year-old Cynthia to live in Dayton. Rhea Stouffer goes along as housekeeper and child-care provider. During this time, George is listed as a driver for a Dayton food services company.

In October, Rhea takes Cynthia back home to Loudonville to attend the annual village Street Fair. George disappears from Dayton with David, leaving no word of their destination or future plans.

In Springfield, Ralph Workman Jr. marries Louise, a young widow from Nashville, Tennessee, whose sister is his neighbor. Louise moves to Springfield with her children, Danny and Peggy.

In late November or early December, George is in Mobile, Alabama, with David. He makes arrangements for Luella Smith to care for two-year-old David.

1952

In late January, Luella Smith has her last contact with George Laswell regarding his son, David, who is still living in her home.

In May, Luella writes a letter and sends it to a newspaper in Dayton, Ohio, asking whether anyone knows the whereabouts of George Laswell.

The Letter from Alabama is published in the Journal Herald in Dayton.

Ralph Workman Jr. travels to Mobile, meets Luella Smith, and gets David. Ralph and Louise take the child into their home in Springfield, Ohio. From this day forward, he has a permanent family—in fact, two families. He will forever be David Workman.

In Loudonville, Rhea Stouffer retains custody of two-year-old Cynthia.

1954

Mickey Workman from Loudonville, Ohio, marries U.S. Navy Machinist's Mate Gene Workman. They live in Lomita, California, for the remaining year of his military service.

1955

Gene is discharged from the Navy. He and wife Mickey return to Loudonville.

1956

Gene and Mickey legally adopt Cynthia, who is six years old. Their son, Mark, is born. They will have three more children— Carol, Cathy and Cheryl.

1961

Gene Workman receives a letter in Loudonville from George Laswell in San Diego. It is the only known record of George's thoughts / feelings about the events he had set in motion.

1970

David Laswell Workman, age 21, goes to court in Springfield, Ohio, and legally becomes David Workman.

1971

At age 21, Cynthia dies of complications from kidney disease.

1983

In Olympia, Washington, David Workman and his family join a Lutheran church and are introduced to Marilyn and Richard Mueller. Marilyn, it turns out, is from Loudonville, Ohio. As their friendship grows, David learns that her father, Harold Obrecht, was a high school friend and classmate of David's mother, Hortense. David also discovers that Marilyn's brother-in-law is a cousin. From his newfound cousin, David will gain insights into brother Gene's well-earned reputation in Loudonville, and will learn about Edna and Clarence Beck, who were David's baptismal sponsors.

2002

David Workman comes into possession of George Laswell's 1961 letter to Gene Workman.

2010

David learns of George Laswell's 1966 death, and begins to reconstruct more details of George's life.

David makes contact with the Rev. Sam Laswell, a first cousin. They establish a mutually rewarding relationship, and David begins to learn the history of his Laswell-Clark-Abney family roots.

David makes contact with Carl Smith, a grandson of Luella Smith, in Mobile, Alabama. They forge a long-distance friendship as Carl helps David to know the woman who cared for him and who wrote the Letter from Alabama—the document that made all the difference in David's life.

Ohio Roots

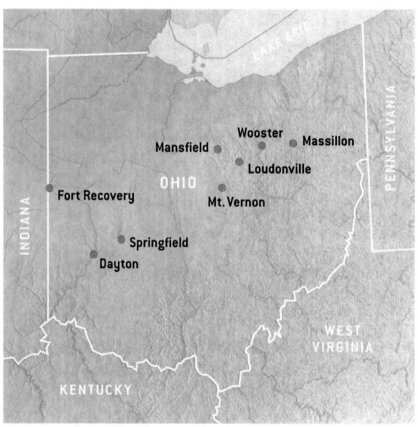

These Ohio towns and cities are where many
of the events in the lives of the Workman and
Laswell families took place

Kentucky Roots

David learned that generations of his birth father's family lived
in and around Rockcastle and Lincoln counties, including
Mount Vernon and Kings Mountain

Bringing David Home

On May 23, 1952, David boarded a train in Mobile with the big man who would change his life. They made their way to the little boy's new home and new family.

Bibliography and Sources

The author is indebted to many researchers and writers whose works helped him re-create the story of *Letter from Alabama*, and the times in which the events occurred.

• First and foremost, the Internet opened the way to much discovery of events long forgotten, or obscured by the mists of time past.

• The Washington State Department of Veterans Affairs and the Kentucky State Department of Veterans Affairs opened a key window into the life of George S. Laswell by providing to his birth son a copy of George's 1943 certificate of honorable discharge from the U.S. Army. This duplicate record is a most fortunate gift, since the original records were destroyed, along with 16 million to 18 million others, in a fire at the National Personnel Records Center.

• Jeanne Yoakam, a Loudonville, Ohio, native, produced a valuable biographical compilation called "Pioneers of the Loudonville Area" in 2000. It is available in the local public library. Jeanne was very kind and helpful in providing obituaries of members of the author's Loudonville-area extended family. Through her efforts, David learned much about ancestors who had existed for him in name only.

• Rachel in the Loudonville Public Library's Local History/Genealogy section, and Sarah in the Ashland, Ohio, Library's Adult Services Department, were very helpful in locating copies of previously unseen family obituaries.

• Wright State University Libraries, Special Collections and Archives, is the owner and custodian of the archives of the Dayton Daily News and the Journal Herald. The author was grateful to be able to purchase electronic copies of 1949 and 1952 editions of newspapers that were essential in retelling the story of *Letter from Alabama*.

- Susan Leininger is a meticulous researcher, genealogist and historian of the many Alsatian-American families in Holmes, Wayne and Ashland counties of Ohio. More than anyone else, she has helped the author to know his Alsatian ancestry and ancestors.

- Jeff Renner is the author of *Three Springs and a Wilderness Station,* a history of the early settlement of what is now Mount Vernon, Kentucky. He kindly answered questions about the early Laswell-Clark-Abney (and related) settlers who followed the Wilderness Road into the Kentucky frontier in the late 1700s.

- In 2002, the Lincoln County, Kentucky, Historical Society published a local history with numerous photos and descriptive articles provided by local families. These include the large extended family of Dr. William David Laswell and his three beloved wives—Letia Cumile, who died soon after childbirth; Eunice, who died in childbirth; and Lucille, who survived him after his death in 1945. For the author of *Letter from Alabama*, the Lincoln County book has become the equivalent of a family photo album of his Kentucky family.

- A web-available history, *The U.S. / American Automobile Industry in World War Two / WWII,* by David D. Jackson, includes an electronic copy of "Frigidaire at War 1944." This website and the Frigidaire book provide a detailed account of how America produced the arms and materials needed to win the epic conflict.

- The helpful source *Dayton History Books Online* (daytonhistorybooks.com) provides a glimpse into life in Dayton during World War II, including the conversion of numerous factories to war production, the expansion of the military air fields that became today's Wright-Paterson Air Force Base, and the construction of emergency wartime housing (including Overlook Homes) for war-production workers.

• Newspapers.com's subscription newspaper archive made it possible for the author to view, for the first time, the 1966 obituary of George S. Laswell, published in the Fresno Bee newspaper.

• Ancestry.com's subscription newspaper archive enabled the author to locate electronic copies of the Mansfield News Journal for the fateful days of March 23-24, 1950—dates which set in motion the events described in *Letter from Alabama*.

• The Morning News Tribune in Tacoma, Washington, employed David Workman as a reporter, editor and columnist for five and a half years in the 1980s. Leading up to the state's 1989 centennial, the Tribune published a coffee-table book, *Washington: A Centennial Portrait,* written by Workman, with compelling photojournalism by Bruce Larson. One of the articles helped the author refresh his memory about the details of one of the wonderful people he met while researching and writing that centennial story.

• In 1977, the Herald newspaper in Everett, Washington, published David Workman's profile of a young woman who was able to reunite with her daughter after seven years without any contact. The newspaper article refreshed the author's memory of specific details of one of the important events recalled in *Letter to Alabama*.

• Old, yellowed newspaper clippings from The Sun in Springfield, Ohio, refreshed the author's memories of his early days as a newspaper reporter.

• The Daily Record newspaper in Wooster, Ohio, published a March 24, 1997, article by Eileen Keller, profiling Gene Workman, a prominent bank officer in Orrville, Ohio.

• Fortunately for David Workman and his family, Ralph O. Workman Sr. allowed his grandson to interview him for several hours in 1984, recalling events and people and experiences that had shaped him and influenced his family. His stories are a window to a time that now goes back more than two centuries.

• A day or so later, Ralph O. Workman Jr. and Gene Workman allowed David to interview the two brothers during a 1984 road trip around Loudonville, Ohio, where they recalled their early lives and family stories in and near the picturesque village. Without their forbearance, these memories would now be lost to the family.

• The author and his family are thankful for a colorful and informative story written by Tom Stafford and published in the Springfield News–Sun on February 3, 1997—celebrating the life of Ralph Workman Jr., who reared and won the love of three children who had lost their fathers.

• Almost everything the author knows about Luella Smith and the home near Mobile, Alabama, he learned from her grandson, Carl—who graciously answered questions, read the manuscript of this story, and provided photos of Luella and the Smith home on Greenleaf Road. The home is no longer standing, and the family photo is a living link to that place.

About the Author

David Workman was a writer and editor at several daily newspapers in Ohio and Washington State. As a journalist, he authored *Washington: A Centennial Portrait*, a book about the state's first 100 years. For several years, he wrote a column published in newspapers around the Pacific Northwest. He then entered public service as communications director for several state agencies in Washington. He was executive editor of state-published books and websites on natural resources, environment, and social and health services. He was a credited contributor to *World Book Encyclopedia*, and a credited source for the *Longstreet Highroad Guide to the Northwest Coast* by Allan and Elizabeth May. He operates Workman & Associates, a communications consulting firm. David and wife Clover enjoy their four children and their families, including six grandchildren. In their free time, they travel and explore.

David and Clover

Notes

[i] Hortense mentioned this in a 1938 letter to her cousin, Irma Monroe, in Fort Recovery, Ohio.

[ii] Wooster, Ohio, Daily Record, March 24, 1997, article by Eileen Keller

[iii] Dayton History Books Online:
http://www.daytonhistorybooks.com/page/page/1652479.htm

[iv] From "Frigidaire at War 1944," produced by the Frigidaire division of General Motors; this book is included in a web-available history, *The U.S. / American Automobile Industry in World War Two / WWII*, by David D. Jackson

[v] Dayton History Books Online:
http://www.daytonhistorybooks.com/page/page/1652479.htm

[vi] Dayton History Books Online:
http://www.daytonhistorybooks.com/page/page/1652479.htm

[vii] 1951 Dayton City Directory

[viii] George S. Laswell, Army of the United States Honorable Discharge record, November 19, 1943

[ix] The Year 1949 From The People History:
http://www.thepeoplehistory.com/1949.html

[x] Ralph Workman Sr. interview with the author, David Workman, in 1984

[xi] Although Wikipedia entries must be treated cautiously, the entry on the Flxible Company holds up well under scrutiny: http://en.wikipedia.org/wiki/Flxible

[xii] Farmer's Almanac:
http://farmersalmanac.com/weather/2012/11/19/the-storm-of-the-century/

[xiii]The original text is "Grandfather's house." For example, see:
http://www.hymnsandcarolsofchristmas.com/Hymns_and_Carols/over_the_river_grandfather.htm

[xiv] http://www.history.com/topics/korean-war

[xv] http://en.m.wikipedia.org/wiki/Collier's

[xvi] Roz Young, 1992 article in the Dayton Daily News republished in Dayton History Books Online: http://www.daytonhistorybooks.com/nuturing.html

[xvii] The author believes Denny's dad said words to this effect, there at water's edge. However, not wanting to put words into his mouth after the passage of a half century, David reflects these words as his own impression.

[xviii] Wooster, Ohio, Daily Record, March 24, 1997, article by Eileen Keller

[xix] For those who have forgotten, or never experienced, how long-distance calls were placed before the "Age of Online Everything," a good overview long-distance land-line phone calling can be found in "Atlanta Telephone History": http://www.atlantatelephonehistory.info/part4.html

[xx] Lincoln County, Kentucky, a 2002 history, published by the Lincoln County Historical Society, Page 216

[xxi] Many Laswell family photos and family stories are found in: Lincoln County, Kentucky, a 2002 history published by the Lincoln County Historical Society

[xxii] History of Kentucky, William Elsey Connelly and E.M. Coulter, Volume V of five volumes, 1922

[xxiii] "–30–" was a traditional way for newspaper journalists to end their stories or articles when submitting them to editors for review. It meant "the end."

[xxiv] Springfield News–Sun, February 3, 1997, Pages 9 and 12, Tom Stafford

CPSIA information can be obtained at www.ICGtesting.com
Printed in the USA
LVOW10s0725210615

443260LV00025B/450/P